PEACE,
LOVE,
and
PASTA

PEACE, LOVE, *and* PASTA

Simple *and* Elegant Recipes *from a* Chef's Home Kitchen

SCOTT CONANT

ABRAMS, NEW YORK

To Meltem, Ayla, and Karya:
You are my world

In Praise of Simplicity

For the first twenty years of my career, everything was complicated: Business was complicated; my life was complicated; my schedule was complicated. Even the food I served in the restaurants was complicated. From my very first kitchen job, I have worked tirelessly to prove myself and discover my own way of doing things. A simpler way. I'm the middle child, so perhaps that's why I've always strived to stand out. But whatever I did, I didn't just want to cook my version of someone else's food.

Becoming a chef was, technically, the backup plan. After my dream career of becoming a professional baseball player and retiring at forty didn't look like it was going to pan out, I turned to vocational school, where I selected plumbing as my initial field of study. (The salaries in most of the other fields topped out at $30,000 a year, but plumbing paid $35K, and I was saving up to buy a car. What can I say? Fifteen-year-old boys have their priorities.) From there, I went to the second choice on my list: culinary arts. (Hairdressing was number three, because that just seemed fun.) Though I had fond associations with cooking and eating from my childhood (the pot of sauce my mother had on the stove every Sunday; sitting around the table after a family dinner watching the adults eat angel wing cookies and pass a bottle of Strega around; lobster rolls with my grandfather in Maine), I hadn't necessarily thought of those memories as prerequisites for a job. But I liked to eat, and I also needed to work. Cooking seemed like something I could do.

I realized I had found my niche after our neighbor Kathy Vitone, one of my mom's close friends, helped me get a job as a dishwasher at the seafood restaurant her husband owned. In the kitchen at the Sea Loft, I rediscovered the atmosphere I had been missing from the baseball field. Over the course of thousands of two-for-one lobster dinners and countless vats of Ritz cracker stuffing and potato salad, I absorbed the close camaraderie, specialization of roles, high stakes, and risk of failure that were familiar to me from my ball-playing years. (Plus, plenty of crazy antics with my teammates behind the scenes.) It's also where I encountered my first mentor, a line cook named Mo Collins, from whom I learned important lessons on how to run a successful kitchen: how to be organized and efficient, and how to keep the mood light even when cooking for large, demanding crowds.

My education in food came next. First at the Sheraton banquet hall in Waterbury, then at San Domenico in New York and at the Hotel Bayerischer Hof in Munich, I started to really pay attention to what I was cooking. My range of ingredients expanded, my technique became more refined, and I started to appreciate how the layering of clean, strong flavors in a dish could elevate it to become more than the sum of its parts. While I lived in Germany, I went to Italy every chance I got and saw how much more there was there food-wise beyond what I knew from the Italian-American cooking I had grown up with, and I fell in love with it. In particular, *cucina rustica*—Italian home cooking—really resonated with me. It was a real light bulb moment: my discovery that rustic, modest, simple dishes could have an elegance that surpassed fussier, more complicated staples of what was then considered fine dining. The key, I realized, was in the elevation of simple elements: a beautiful fish cooked in a straightforward way, or perfectly ripe tomatoes accompanied by only fresh basil, burrata, and extra-virgin olive oil. By the time I returned to New York, in the mid-1990s, and eventually made my way to Chianti (the Upper East Side restaurant I helmed after leaving San Domenico), I was champing at the bit to start communicating this message, through my cooking, to the world.

Chianti was the first kitchen that was really my own, and I gave all of myself to it: all of my creativity and passion in the kitchen, and whatever remaining energy I could summon making the rounds in the dining room every night. It was exhausting. Whenever I wasn't working, I was constantly panicked that people weren't going to get what I was trying to say: that there are so many amazing things that can be done with simple ingredients treated right, that "rustic" cooking doesn't have to mean "sloppy." But in 1998, somebody did: Ruth Reichl gave us a great review in the *New York Times*, praising the "admirable simplicity" of the food. That review, and the success of Chianti, propelled me toward new opportunities in restaurants, TV, and retail—opportunities that were very exciting but, increasingly, made my life busier and more complicated professionally, just as I was ready to focus on my previously neglected personal life.

During this period, I got married, my daughters were born, and I moved out of New York. Little by little, my life shifted in a way where, for the first time in decades, I was cooking primarily for the people I loved, and my goal was no longer to impress this new clientele so much as it was to nourish them and spend time with them around the table. And simultaneously came the introduction, through my wife, Mel, to Turkey and

Turkish cooking. All of a sudden, I was falling in love with an entirely new cuisine, one that I soon felt a kinship with—however poor my Turkish language skills were—because of its reverence for clean, clear flavors and the value my wife's family put on spending time around the table together. This emphasis only increased when our girls, Ayla and Karya, came along, and it has deepened as I've seen how we are all folded into the family through the mealtime rituals and our discovery together of this world of new tastes. Let me tell you, there's nothing like a Turkish breakfast table to make you feel part of a family.

Over the course of my career, I've come to think of simplicity as the ultimate luxury, but also an attainable one. The recipes here sometimes require a little patience, sometimes require seeking out a particular ingredient, but they aren't complicated. The goal of each is to deliver a precise balance of flavors, and to satisfy everyone at the table (a skill I have gained much experience with in recent years, given that my younger daughter, Karya, is a classic picky eater). This book is particularly special to me because of the connection I have to the recipes as both chef and audience—these are the recipes that are closest to my heart because I've drawn on my greatest hits and favorite cooking memories from throughout my career to create dishes that I can share at home with my family, and through these dishes, share those experiences with them.

In my house, it's not unusual for me to hear banter (or bickering) in Turkish that I don't fully understand as Mel tries to immerse the girls in their second language. Food is *my* second language, and I am trying to make sure my girls become fluent in that as well, by bringing them into the kitchen with me and exposing them to the magical transformation of ingredients through cooking. My hope is that, through the recipes in this book, you can do the same.

CHAPTER 1

Simple Staples

Small but mighty is how I think of the recipes in this chapter—secret weapons of flavor that kick things up a notch when deployed in everyday cooking. All of these sauces and condiments can be used on a variety of dishes—pasta, sandwiches, with vegetables or meat, or as snacking dips—which is why they're great staples for any home kitchen. Most of the recipes are based on preparations that I've taken with me from restaurant to restaurant, things I have always been able to rely on as flavor enhancers that I've kept in my back pocket. As for how to use them, there really are no rules. You can pick one and experiment with different uses for it over the course of a week (most of these keep at least a week in the fridge or pantry), or do what I do and keep the entire arsenal at the ready so whether it's crunch, umami, freshness, or acidity you're after at any given moment, you always have what you need to make your food really shine.

HORSERADISH AGLIATA

Agliata is a savory, garlic- and breadcrumb-based condiment popular in the region of Liguria on Italy's northwestern coast. This version, which includes an additional kick of horseradish and the rounded flavor of thrice-blanched garlic, is based on a sauce for beef ravioli that I've had on my menus for years. At home, I often use it on short ribs and baked oysters; it's my go-to whenever I'm looking for an assertive flavor.

Prep Note: This recipe requires a minimum of 1 hour of chilling time.

Makes 2 cups (about 500 g)

¾ cup (180 g) Prepared Horseradish (recipe follows)

⅔ cup (55 g) panko

3 cloves garlic, blanched three times

¼ cup (60 ml) extra-virgin olive oil

Pinch crushed red pepper

Pinch kosher salt, plus additional as needed to taste

IN A MIXING BOWL, combine the horseradish and panko and let sit for 5 minutes. Put the horseradish-panko mixture in a blender with the garlic, red pepper flakes, salt, and ½ cup (120 ml) plus 2 tablespoons water and purée until smooth. Gradually add the oil and continue to blend until emulsified. Chill in the refrigerator for at least an hour before serving, or until it's chilled all the way through. The agliata will last for up to a week, stored in an airtight container in the refrigerator.

Prepared Horseradish

Makes ¾ cup (180 g)

½ cup (120 g) peeled and finely sliced horseradish root

¼ cup (60 ml) distilled white vinegar

Pinch salt, plus more as needed

Put the horseradish, vinegar, and salt in a blender, then add enough water to just cover the horseradish. Blend until smooth, then taste and add more salt if needed. (The horseradish flavor should be very strong.) Stored in an airtight container, the prepared horseradish will last in the fridge for several months.

VEGGIE BOMBA

Forget chickpeas: Bomba is my hummus. Bursting with the flavors and textures of all the different vegetables—*bomba* means "bomb" in Italian—this is a foolproof, crowd-pleasing spread or dip for bread, chips, and vegetables. (It is also a nice accompaniment for cheese.) This Calabrian condiment has infinite iterations, though I prefer it with a chunky texture rather than perfectly smooth. And it's a great way to get the most out of your produce haul: It lasts for a week in the fridge, and you can customize with whatever vegetables you have on hand.

Note: I roast the vegetables in a convection oven because I like the effect the air circulation has on the roasting, but if you don't have one at home, you can roast them in a regular oven; just increase the heat by 25°F (15°C).

Makes 2½ cups (560 g)

1 large eggplant, peeled and roughly diced

1½ cups (225 g) peeled and roughly diced fresh artichokes

1 red bell pepper, diced

2 whole mild cherry peppers, stems removed

4 cloves garlic, crushed

½ cup (80 g) green olives, pitted (I use castelvetrano)

6 tablespoons (90 ml) extra-virgin olive oil

1½ teaspoons fennel seeds, toasted and ground

¼ tablespoon crushed red pepper

¼ cup (10 g) roughly chopped fresh basil leaves

Kosher salt

Zest and juice of ¼ lemon

PREHEAT A CONVECTION OVEN TO 375°F (190°C). (If using a regular oven, preheat to 400°F [205°C].) Place the eggplant, artichokes, red pepper, cherry pepper, garlic, and olives in a large bowl. Add 2 tablespoons of the olive oil, the fennel seeds, and red pepper flakes and toss until well coated.

On a large cookie sheet, arrange the vegetables in a single layer and roast until the skins of the vegetables are golden and the flesh is soft enough to purée, about 25 minutes. Remove the pan to a wire rack and let the vegetables cool.

Place the cooled vegetables in a food processor and pulse while drizzling in the remaining 4 tablespoons (60 ml) olive oil until the mixture is midway between smooth and rough. (The final product should be spreadable, but not completely puréed.) Stir in the basil and season with salt to taste. The bomba will keep for a week, stored in an airtight container in the fridge.

BROCCOLI RABE PESTO

This recipe is a tried-and-true crowd-pleaser: Everyone who tastes it wants to know how come I haven't tried to bottle it. But the answer (and the key to its addictive flavor) is the fresh taste of the broccoli rabe, which isn't cooked. It's great on pasta for sure, but I love it on sandwiches, grilled or roasted chicken, roasted pork, or even a grilled skirt steak. Honestly, you may just want to open the jar and eat it out of the container with a spoon.

Makes 3 cups (720 ml)

1 bunch broccoli rabe, roughly chopped

2 cloves garlic, whole and unpeeled

⅔ cup (150 ml) extra-virgin olive oil

5 tablespoons (30 g) grated Parmigiano-Reggiano cheese

4 tablespoons (60 g) chopped Pickled Fresno Chiles (recipe follows), plus ¼ cup (60 ml) of the pickling liquid

Kosher salt

IN A FOOD PROCESSOR, combine the broccoli rabe with the garlic and olive oil and pulse until the rabe is coarsely chopped.

Remove the mixture from the food processor, place in a bowl, and mix in the cheese, chiles, and pickling liquid. Season with salt to taste and serve immediately, or transfer to an airtight container and refrigerate. The pesto will last for 4 to 5 days, stored in an airtight container in the refrigerator.

Pickled Fresno Chiles

In addition to making them for the pesto, I also use these chiles in the Chicken Cutlet Sandwich on page 164, the Tuna Crudo on page 110, on top of guacamole, or as an accompaniment to fried chicken—they're a great addition to any dish that needs a hit of acid.

Makes 2 cups chiles, plus pickling liquid

Prep Note: This recipe requires several hours (or overnight) to chill completely before serving.

2 cups sliced Fresno chiles, with seeds

1 cup (240 ml) white wine vinegar

¾ cup (150 g) sugar

1 tablespoon kosher salt

1 teaspoon coriander seeds, toasted and crushed

1 teaspoon crushed red pepper

Place the chiles and their seeds in a large airtight container with a tight-fitting lid. In a saucepan, combine 2 cups water (480 ml), the vinegar, sugar, salt, coriander, and red pepper flakes and bring to a boil. Pour the boiling liquid into the container with the chiles and cover. Let the jar cool to room temperature, then place in the fridge overnight, or until completely chilled, before using. The pickled chiles will keep in the fridge for up to 2 months.

EGGPLANT CAPONATA

My Italian grandmother made caponata, though of course, being from Italy, she never followed a recipe. So when I developed my own, I tried to capture the particular flavors and textures of her version from memory. This caponata recipe, which I would say is loosely based on how she made it, has been on menus at my restaurants since the dawn of time (or at least it feels that way). People love it because the taste is so complex—customers sometimes ask to buy a quart to take with them, and I sell it to them when they do—but it's actually quite easy to make at home. (The key to the depth of the flavor is deep-frying the eggplant, then tossing it in the sauce afterward.) Use it on bread, as an antipasto, or as a condiment. It will keep for up to 10 days in an airtight container in the fridge, though mine is usually eaten up well before then. If you're short on time, you can make this recipe without salting the eggplant first, but salting it to extract excess liquid makes it much easier to fry.

Makes 2 cups

1 large eggplant (about 1 pound/455 g), cut into 1-inch (2.5 cm) cubes (about 2½ cups)

1 teaspoon kosher salt, plus more to taste

2 tablespoons extra-virgin olive oil, plus more for frying the eggplant

1 small onion, diced

2 cloves garlic, thinly sliced

1 tablespoon capers, preferably salt-packed, well rinsed

Pinch crushed red pepper

1½ cups (360 ml) Pomodoro Sauce (page 64), or good-quality store-bought tomato sauce

1 teaspoon chopped fresh oregano

10 basil leaves, thinly sliced

¼ cup pine nuts, toasted until golden

TOSS THE EGGPLANT with the kosher salt in a colander. Put the colander in a clean sink, and then weight the cubes of eggplant by placing a plate or the lid of a pot directly on top, and a saucepan of water on top of the plate or lid. Allow the salt to draw out the excess moisture from the eggplant, 30 to 40 minutes.

Meanwhile, heat the olive oil in a medium saucepan over medium heat. Add the onion, garlic, capers, red pepper flakes, and a pinch of salt. Sauté until the onion is tender and light brown, about 7 minutes. Add the tomato sauce and oregano and stir to combine. Reduce the heat to low, cover the pan, and cook until the tomato sauce reduces somewhat and the flavors have melded, about 20 minutes. Keep warm while you fry the eggplant.

After the eggplant has released its excess liquid, pat it dry. In a large, high-sided sauté pan over medium-high, heat enough olive oil to cover the eggplant cubes by about ¼ inch. Working in batches to make sure there is room between the cubes, fry the eggplant in the sauté pan, stirring occasionally, until well browned and tender on all sides, 7 to 10 minutes per batch, transferring each batch to a paper towel–lined plate as you go. Add more oil as needed between batches, as the eggplant will soak it up like a sponge.

Stir the basil into the tomato sauce. Return all of the eggplant to the sauté pan and reduce the heat to low. Add just enough of the tomato sauce to the eggplant so the mixture is the consistency of a chunky stew. (Any leftover tomato sauce can be saved and served over pasta.) Cool to room temperature, taste, and season again. Toss in the pine nuts just before serving.

ROASTED GARLIC, PARMIGIANO-REGGIANO, AND EVOO SPREAD

This recipe was born out of the by-products of another one of my signature staples: pomodoro sauce. When we made the sauce at the restaurants, we were always left with a pot of garlic cooked in olive oil that I couldn't bear to waste. So I started taking those delicious leftovers, adding a little more olive oil and Parmigiano-Reggiano, and turning it into a spread. If you are making the Pomodoro Sauce (page 64), you can do the same thing—or you can make this spread from scratch using the recipe below.

Makes 1½ cups

2 heads garlic, cloves peeled

¼ teaspoon crushed red pepper

1 cup (240 ml) plus 1 tablespoon extra-virgin olive oil

1 tablespoon roughly chopped fresh flat-leaf parsley

1⅓ cups (130 g) grated Parmigiano-Reggiano cheese

Kosher salt

PLACE THE GARLIC AND RED PEPPER FLAKES in a saucepan and cover with 1 tablespoon of the olive oil. Cook over very low heat until the garlic is golden and soft.

Place the garlic and its cooking oil in a food processor and blend until puréed. Transfer the garlic mixture to a serving bowl, then add the parsley and cheese, and stir to combine. Pour the remaining 1 cup (240 ml) olive oil around the garlic mixture and season with salt to your liking. Serve immediately, or refrigerate until ready to use: The finished recipe will keep in the refrigerator for 3 days, or the cooked garlic will hold for up to 1 week, with the parsley, Parmesan, and oil added just before serving.

GREMOLATA

Gremolata is traditionally served with osso bucco; at the restaurants, I used to like to take the bone marrow from inside of the veal shank, lightly poach it so that it was still pink in the center, then combine it with the gremolata and serve that with the osso bucco tableside. But it's just as delicious without that showmanship, and incredibly versatile. I use this on grilled fish, seafood such as scallops, roast chicken, and pasta. What distinguishes my gremolata recipe from others are the pickled alliums, which add a bright acidity. You can change up these alliums and herbs depending on what you have on hand. Pickled leeks, garlic, shallot, and onion work well, and you can add a pinch of another chopped herb like rosemary or tarragon to customize the flavor profile to whatever you are cooking.

Makes 1 cup (240 ml)

¼ cup (60 ml) extra-virgin olive oil

1 clove garlic

½ cup (25 g) finely chopped fresh Italian parsley

2 tablespoons pine nuts, toasted

6 tablespoons (90 ml) Pickled Ramps (recipe follows) or another pickled allium, such as leeks or green onions

1 teaspoon lemon zest

Flaky sea salt

HEAT THE OLIVE OIL in a small saucepan over low heat. Using a microplane grater, grate the garlic into the oil and let it warm gently for 5 minutes, adjusting the heat to prevent it from coloring.

Transfer the garlic and oil to a bowl and add the parsley, pine nuts, pickled leeks, and lemon zest. Season to taste with sea salt and serve immediately, or let the gremolata warm to room temperature, cover, and refrigerate. As long as the parsley is submerged in oil, this will keep in the refrigerator for 3 or 4 days.

Pickled Ramps

If ramps are not available, another allium (such as leeks or green onions) can be substituted.

Makes 1 quart (960 ml)

Prep Note: This recipe requires several hours (or overnight) to chill before serving.

1 cup (240 ml) rice wine vinegar

1 cup (240 ml) Champagne vinegar

1⅓ cups (265 g) sugar

1½ tablespoons crushed red pepper

1½ tablespoons coriander seeds

1 whole star anise

1 whole clove

1 Szechuan black peppercorn

1 tablespoon whole black peppercorns

1 bay leaf

1 teaspoon sea salt

1½ cups fresh ramps, cleaned and trimmed, leaves removed

In a small saucepan, combine the vinegars, 1 cup (240 ml) water, the sugar, red pepper flakes, coriander seeds, star anise, clove, peppercorns, bay leaf, and sea salt. Bring to a boil, then reduce the heat and simmer for 10 minutes.

Place the ramps in a heat-safe container with a tight-fitting lid. Pour the liquid over the ramps and allow them to cool to room temperature, then cover and refrigerate at least overnight before use. (The pickled ramps will keep in the refrigerator for several months.)

SOFFRITTO

Soffritto is the backbone of so much of my cooking, even, or especially, when I'm trying to make something on the fly. Unlike most of the recipes in this chapter—which I use to bump up the flavor of dishes after cooking—soffritto is a foundation that gives depth to whatever is cooked in it. Often used as a base for soups, stews, sauces, and stocks, it elevates even the simplest ingredients to become more than the sum of their parts. If I want to make a quick soup, for instance, I'll put this soffritto in the bottom of the pot, add cauliflower and chicken broth, simmer, and that's it. Or if I find a bunch of great-looking vegetables at the market that I don't really have a plan for, I'll buy 'em and then cook them with this. My soffritto doesn't include carrots and celery, as would be traditional, because I don't like it to have the flavor of any particular vegetable; I want it to fortify whatever else I'm cooking. It's less about adding a specific flavor and more about enhancing the flavor of your other ingredients—I like to think of it as the soul of the dish.

Makes about 3 cups

2 cups finely diced shallots (about 6 to 8 medium shallots)

2 tablespoons minced fresh garlic

¼ teaspoon crushed red pepper

1 cup (240 ml) extra-virgin olive oil

1 teaspoon kosher salt

IN A LARGE SAUTÉ PAN, heat the olive oil on medium heat and add the shallots, garlic, and red pepper flakes. Sweat them with the kosher salt until most of the moisture is evaporated and the shallots are translucent, 7 to 10 minutes. (Reduce the heat to low, if necessary, to prevent the garlic from burning.) You can add other ingredients to the soffritto and start cooking with it immediately, or save in an airtight container in the fridge until ready to use, or up to 6 days.

A FEW OTHER PANTRY ITEMS AND TIPS

BUTTER

Always cook with unsalted butter; it gives you more control over the amount of salt that's added during the cooking process.

BROTH/STOCK

With the exception of the lobster stock used in the Pici with Lobster (page 81) and Stuffed Lobster (page 116), I typically use store-bought broths and stocks when I cook at home. I recommend looking for high-quality organic brands, and low-sodium varieties if you want more control over salting.

OLIVE OIL

Though the type of olive oil is specified in the ingredient list of each recipe, I almost always use extra-virgin olive oil. (With the exception of some of the dishes that are fried, which call for vegetable oil.)

SALT

I use kosher salt in almost all of my cooking except occasionally for finishing a dish, when I call for a flaky sea salt, such as Maldon.

SPECIAL INGREDIENTS

All of the special ingredients called for in this book, such as the yufka dough, the pul biber, the Turkish red pepper paste, the neonata, the Calabrian chiles, and the black caraway seeds, are widely available online and in specialty stores, and I encourage you to seek out anything that is specifically called for, as it will make the dish that much better. I swear by a line of professional-grade sauces, stocks, and demi-glaces called More than Gourmet, so their items are called out occasionally as well.

SPECIAL EQUIPMENT

A stand mixer with a whisk and dough-hook attachments is useful for the fresh pasta recipes and other doughs called for in this book. Pasta-making attachments for the stand mixer are nice too. A pasta roller is also very helpful for some of those recipes (though not imperative). And if you enjoy ravioli, consider investing in stamps or molds, which will make the filling and cutting process much easier.

A kitchen thermometer and an instant-read thermometer are useful for deep-frying and for meat recipes, respectively. (Though I actually use a regular infrared thermometer to take the temperature of oil before frying.) A meat mallet is needed for the cutlet recipes, of which there are a few.

SALSA VERDE

Not to be confused with a Mexican salsa verde (*salsa verde* means "green sauce" in both languages), the Italian version is pungent rather than spicy, thanks to the olives, capers, cornichons, and anchovies; it also has a note of freshness from the puréed parsley. Traditionally served with bollito misto (a northern Italian dish of mixed boiled meats), this bright, bracing sauce pairs well with hearty meats, but it also works on pretty much any dish that needs a kick of acid. (As with the Gremolata on page 20, I like it with fish and roast chicken.) The recipe below is a good staple, but you can also experiment with swapping in different soft herbs (fennel fronds, tarragon, chives), a mix of different olives, or other pickled vegetables.

Makes 3 cups

½ cup (42 g) cocktail onions, drained

3 anchovy fillets, rinsed well (optional)

1 tablespoon capers, drained and washed well

1 cup (155 g) pitted green olives

¼ cup (40 g) cornichons

1 cup (240 ml) extra-virgin olive oil

½ bunch flat-leaf parsley, tough stems removed

COMBINE THE COCKTAIL ONIONS, anchovies, capers, olives, and cornichons in a blender and blend until smooth. Transfer the mixture to a clean bowl.

Rinse the blender, then add the oil and parsley and blend until just smooth. (Do not blend for too long or the mixture might get hot, which causes the parsley to darken.)

Add the parsley purée to the onion-caper mixture and combine with a rubber spatula or wooden spoon. Serve immediately at room temperature, or refrigerate. The salsa verde will last for up to 1 week in the refrigerator, but it's best within 3 days, before the parsley has marinated for too long.)

WALNUT VINAIGRETTE

This is the dressing I always have in my fridge: a straightforward vinaigrette elevated by the depth of flavor of the walnut oil. Walnut oil is one of my favorite ingredients, not so much because I like the flavor of walnuts themselves but because of its powerful aroma, which fills in the gaps in a simple combination of ingredients like olive oil and vinegar. Dress the greens of your choice with the vinaigrette, then top with about ½ cup (60 g) chopped walnuts.

Makes 2½ cups (600 ml)

¼ cup (60 ml) balsamic vinegar

¼ cup (60 ml) red wine vinegar

Kosher salt

1 cup (240 ml) walnut oil

1 cup (240 ml) extra-virgin olive oil

COMBINE THE VINEGARS and a little bit of salt in a bowl. Slowly whisk in the walnut and extra-virgin olive oils. This dressing can last in an airtight container covered with a tight-fitting lid for up to 1 month in the fridge.

Simple Staples

TOGARASHI-INSPIRED SUNFLOWER SPICE

In Italy, I encountered a lot of Japanese chefs, and I learned that many spend years working there to learn the heart and soul of Italian cooking before returning to open Italian restaurants back home. Years later, I took a trip to Japan, and what I found there blew my mind: The mastery of Italy's deep, soulful approach to cooking combined with a Japanese reverence for food and presentation was magical.

This recipe is my homage to those chefs. It's a riff on togarashi, a complex hot-and-sweet blend of chiles and a variety of other seasonings that you sprinkle on dishes to give them a kick. The traditional preparation is more of a spice, while my version includes the crunch of sunflower and pumpkin seeds to give it texture and body. I often throw this on top of salads and pasta; it's particularly good on a filled pasta that has enough surface area to catch the crumbs. (Try it over pumpkin ravioli—the addition of spice combines beautifully with pumpkin's natural sweetness.)

Makes 2 cups (375 g)

1 cup (80 g) panko

½ cup (140 g) hulled sunflower seeds

½ cup (65 g) hulled pumpkin seeds

2 to 3 tablespoons vegetable oil

Kosher salt and Aleppo pepper (see Special Ingredients, page 23)

¼ to ½ cup Twice-Blanched Garlic Chips (recipe follows)

ADD THE PANKO CRUMBS to a small dry skillet set over medium-low heat. Stir the panko with a wooden spoon, distributing the crumbs evenly around the pan, for about 5 minutes, or until the crumbs are golden brown. (Watch the crumbs carefully as you stir to prevent the ones on the edges of the pan from burning.) Remove from heat and set aside.

Wipe out the skillet, then add the sunflower and pumpkin seeds with the oil and toast over medium heat, watching carefully, until the seeds are very fragrant and golden brown on the exterior, 7 to 8 minutes. Remove from heat, place the seeds on a paper towel to drain the oil, then salt to taste. Reserve the oil from the pan.

Combine the panko, seeds, and garlic chips in a bowl and toss with some of the reserved oil. Add more salt, if needed, and Aleppo pepper to taste. The oil will add some flavor, but the mixture should not be wet. Keep in an airtight container, at room temperature, for up to 3 weeks.

Twice-Blanched Garlic Chips

Makes about ¼ cup (60 g) chips

4 cloves garlic, peeled

½ cup (120 ml) cold water

1 cup (240 ml) vegetable oil

Kosher salt

Slice the garlic with a mandolin, or if you'd prefer to use a sharp chef's knife, slice the cloves about 1 mm thick. Place the raw garlic slices in a pot and cover with the cold water. Bring to a boil, then drain. Repeat the blanching process once more.

Place the twice-blanched garlic in a heavy-bottomed pot and cover the cloves with the oil. Heat over medium-high heat and fry until the garlic is light golden brown and crisp, 10 to 15 minutes.

Remove the garlic slices from the oil with a spider or serrated spoon and place on paper towels to drain. Lightly salt before using. The garlic chips can be made up to 7 days ahead and stored in a dry environment in an airtight container over a layer of paper towels.

CHAPTER 2

A Few Things for the Morning

Full confession: I'm not a breakfast person. Coffee, yes—the sooner the better. But a meal in the morning isn't really my thing. What can I say? I've worked in restaurants for way too long.

Now that I'm mostly cooking for a family audience rather than a fine-dining one, though, I've got a constituency of small eaters (my two daughters) that needs to have something in the morning, and this has inspired me to get breakfast dishes back in my repertoire. Some of the recipes in this chapter—such as the Gianduja French Toast and the Lemon Ricotta Pancakes (pages 31 and 34)—are adapted from stints I've had over the years at establishments with a breakfast or brunch service. Others—like the frittata (page 32), or the Polenta Waffles (page 35)—are technically breakfast menu items but work well at any time of day, in my opinion. Personally, if I'm not making breakfast for the girls, I'm fine with a little slice of one of the baked goods in chapter 10, like the hazelnut cake, the plum tart, or biscotti—basically anything that you can pair with coffee sounds like a good breakfast to me. But for mornings that call for heartier fare or on weekends when you want to make breakfast a real family meal, these recipes are my go-tos.

FRENCH TOAST WITH GIANDUJA WHIPPED CREAM

My daughters are not huge fans of French toast, but Nutella can be very persuasive—this is one breakfast that everyone in my house can agree on. (*Gianduja* is the general term for chocolate-hazelnut spread, of which Nutella is the most popular brand.) Throughout my career, I've done riffs on French toast at restaurants to make this familiar dish a little more surprising, and this is the one that's stuck. The key is making sure the bread is really well-soaked—if you have time, you could even soak the slices overnight.

Serves 4

6 large eggs

¾ cup (180 ml) milk

¾ cup (180 ml) heavy whipping cream

1 teaspoon vanilla extract

¼ teaspoon ground cinnamon

2 tablespoons maple syrup

8 slices brioche, each 1 inch (2.5 cm) thick

Butter, for the griddle pan

Gianduja Whipped Cream (recipe follows), for serving

Confectioners' sugar, for sprinkling

WHISK THE EGGS IN A MIXING BOWL, then add the milk, cream, vanilla, cinnamon, and maple syrup and whisk to combine.

Soak each piece of bread in the egg mixture until thoroughly saturated, for a minimum of 30 seconds on each side.

Butter a griddle pan and heat to medium-high. Lower the heat to medium, arrange the bread slices on it (depending on the size of your pan, you may have to do this in batches), and fry until the bottom is golden brown, approximately 1 minute. Flip, then fry the other side.

Place two slices of French toast on each plate. Top with a large dollop of the chocolate-hazelnut whipped cream, sprinkle with confectioners' sugar, and serve immediately.

Gianduja Whipped Cream

Makes 2 cups (80 g)

1 cup (240 ml) plus 1 tablespoon heavy whipping cream

¼ cup (75 g) Nutella, or other brand of chocolate-hazelnut spread

Add 1 tablespoon of the cream to the Nutella, and stir until combined. (This will thin the Nutella out, which will make it easier to work with.)

Whip the remaining 1 cup (240 ml) cream until it forms soft peaks, then switch to a rubber spatula and fold in the Nutella mixture. Cover and refrigerate until ready to serve.

ZUCCHINI FRITTATA

I think a frittata is only as good as the things you put in it, so the key to this frittata is getting the zucchini really well browned—it should be a deep golden color. (I prefer smaller zucchini to larger ones, which I find can be too bitter.) This recipe yields a decent-sized frittata, so it's a great thing to make in the morning, then leave out in the kitchen for people to nibble on throughout the day. If you want to make a meal out of it, serve it warm with a salad of butter-head lettuce dressed in the Walnut Vinaigrette on page 25.

Serves 6 to 8

12 large eggs

1 tablespoon chopped fresh parsley

1 tablespoon chopped fresh basil

1 tablespoon thinly sliced fresh chives

2 tablespoons grated Grana Padano or Parmigiano-Reggiano cheese, plus more for serving

½ teaspoon kosher salt, plus more to taste

1 teaspoon freshly ground black pepper

Pinch crushed red pepper

¼ cup (60 ml) extra-virgin olive oil, plus more for finishing

2 pounds (910 g) assorted small zucchini, cut into ⅛-inch-thick rounds

4 shallots, sliced

1 clove garlic, peeled and crushed

1 teaspoon chopped fresh thyme

PREHEAT THE OVEN TO 350°F (175°C). In a mixing bowl, whisk the eggs, then add the parsley, basil, chives, cheese, salt, pepper, and red pepper flakes and whisk again.

In a large nonstick ovenproof skillet, heat the olive oil over medium-high heat. Add the zucchini, shallots, garlic, and thyme, and season generously with salt. Sauté until the zucchini is just tender and nicely browned on both sides.

Add the egg mixture to the skillet. With a rubber spatula, continuously bring the eggs towards the center of the pan until the liquid begins to set, shaking the pan occasionally to distribute the liquid, about 1 minute 45 seconds. Use a spatula to even the surface and edges.

Place the pan in the preheated oven and bake the frittata for 18 to 22 minutes, checking occasionally, until the center stays set when you jiggle the pan.

Remove from oven and place a large plate upside down on the pan, then flip the frittata onto the plate. Drizzle with more olive oil and sprinkle with additional grated cheese. Allow to cool slightly before slicing the frittata into wedges. Serve immediately, or let cool to room temperature first.

LEMON RICOTTA PANCAKES

When I first developed this recipe years ago, the idea of using ricotta in pancakes was fairly novel, and people went crazy for them. Since then, I've tweaked the now-common combination of lemon and ricotta by adding thyme, which gives them a savory dimension that deepens the overall flavor. But what really brings these pancakes over the top is their texture—I whip the egg whites to give them a decadent soufflé-like mouthfeel that makes for an unforgettable breakfast.

Makes about 12 pancakes

¾ cup (95 g) all-purpose flour

2 teaspoons baking powder

½ teaspoon baking soda

1¼ cups (300 ml) milk

3 large eggs, separated, both yolks and whites reserved

¼ cup (½ stick/55 g) unsalted butter, melted, plus more for the griddle

Pinch kosher salt

4½ tablespoons (55 g) sugar

½ teaspoon fresh thyme leaves, roughly chopped

1 teaspoon vanilla extract

Zest of 1 lemon

¾ cup (185 g) ricotta cheese

Maple syrup, lemon curd, or Summer Compote (page 225), for serving

SIFT TOGETHER THE FLOUR, baking powder, and baking soda in a medium bowl.

In a large bowl, whisk together the milk, egg yolks, melted butter, salt, sugar, thyme, vanilla extract, and lemon zest. Sift the dry ingredients into the wet ingredients and gently stir just until combined. Do not overmix.

Using an electric mixer on medium speed, whip the egg whites until they form stiff glossy peaks, about 3 to 4 minutes, taking care not to over whip.

Using a rubber spatula, fold one-third of the egg whites and all the ricotta into the batter, but do not mix it. (You should be able to see streaks of ricotta in the mixture.) Gently fold the remaining egg whites in. The final mixture should have visible streaks of egg white and ricotta, and be very fluffy.

Lightly butter a griddle pan, then heat the pan on medium-low. Working in batches if necessary, ladle about ¼ cup (55 g) batter per pancake onto the griddle pan and cook until bubbles start to form on the top side, 4 to 5 minutes. Flip the pancakes and cook for about 2 minutes on the other side. Place on a serving platter and serve immediately with maple syrup, lemon curd, or some of the compote.

POLENTA WAFFLES

This recipe is an Italian-inspired twist on an American classic: griddled cornbread. Corn-meal (in the form of polenta) gives the batter that extra earthy depth of flavor that I love and a dynamic texture when it comes out of the waffle iron. I love these waffles in the morning with coffee and a ton of butter, but they're also great with a fruit compote, such as the one on page 227.

Note: These waffles call for dry instant polenta, not to be confused with the kind that comes in a tube.

Serves 4 to 6

¾ cup (95 g) plus 2 tablespoons all-purpose flour

2½ tablespoons dry instant polenta

1½ teaspoons baking powder

Pinch kosher salt

2 tablespoons sugar

2½ tablespoons unsalted butter, melted

½ cup (120 ml) milk

½ cup (120 ml) buttermilk

1 teaspoon vanilla extract

2 large eggs, separated, both yolks and whites reserved

WHISK TOGETHER THE FLOUR, polenta, baking powder, salt, and sugar in a mixing bowl.

Stir together the melted butter, milk, buttermilk, and vanilla, then add the wet ingredients to the dry ingredients. Stir until just combined.

In a separate bowl, whip the egg whites with an electric mixer until they form stiff peaks, for 4 to 6 minutes, then gently fold the whipped egg whites into the batter.

Pour the batter into a preheated waffle iron and cook for 6 to 8 minutes, or according to the directions on your waffle maker. (When steam stops coming out of the waffle maker, that's a good indicator that the waffle is done cooking.) Serve immediately.

THREE-EGG OMELET WITH TRIPLE-CREAM CHEESE

I made this for the girls one day and I was just so, so happy to see that they liked triple-cream cheese as much as I do. So now, when I want to ensure they'll be in a good mood for the day, I make them this omelet for breakfast. Note that this recipe does not include any pepper; I have a bit of a beef with black pepper, because I think a lot of people conflate salt and pepper. Salt enhances an ingredient's flavor, whereas pepper has a flavor expression of its own. I'm not a huge fan of black pepper in general, but this dish has such an elegant flavor and subtle texture from the triple-cream cheese that an assertive seasoning like black pepper would totally wreck it. I also am very particular about how I cook my omelets: The cardinal rule of omelets is that they should not take on any color, so stirring the eggs vigorously (and attentively) is crucial.

Makes 1 omelet

3 large eggs

2 tablespoons milk

1 tablespoon unsalted butter

Pinch kosher salt

1 ounce (28 g) triple-cream cheese, such as Brie or Camembert

1 teaspoon chopped fresh chives or chervil (optional), for garnish

PLACE THE EGGS and milk in a blender and blend until smooth.

Melt the butter in a 6-inch (15 cm) nonstick pan on medium-low heat. Pour the egg mixture into the pan, add the salt, and stir very quickly with a wooden spoon. When the egg mixture appears to have small bubbles and looks almost curdled, move the pan around and off the flame so that the eggs cook evenly, but still look wet and haven't taken on any color. Remove from the heat and add the triple-cream cheese in the center. (The residual heat will melt the cheese.)

When ready to serve, place a serving plate on a surface near the stove. Tilt the pan forward at a 45-degree angle (so that the side of the pan that is closest to you is higher than the side further away). Then, using a fork or the wooden spoon with which you stirred the eggs, start to roll the omelet down the pan, folding the egg over itself, until it gets to the edge, then flip it directly onto the plate. (Alternatively, you may flip the omelet in half with a spatula, without tilting the pan, and transfer it to a plate.) Garnish with chives or chervil, if using, and serve immediately.

EGGS IN PURGATORY

Uova in purgatorio is something that was always around at breakfast time on my mother's side of the family, and I've tried to keep up the tradition, mostly because it's so good, and a great way to feed a group. This recipe includes a bit of Calabrian chile, because I like it very spicy—and purgatory is, by definition, a little hot—but it can easily be omitted. As good as it is on its own, it's even better with a hunk of crusty bread dipped in olive oil to lap up all the sauce.

Serves 4 to 6

6 tablespoons (90 ml) extra-virgin olive oil

3 tablespoons thinly sliced garlic

Pinch crushed red pepper

2½ cups (600 ml) Pomodoro Sauce (page 64), or another good-quality tomato sauce

1 tablespoon chopped Calabrian chile (optional)

3 tablespoons chopped fresh flat-leaf parsley

3 tablespoons roughly chopped fresh basil

3 tablespoons finely chopped fresh chives

12 large eggs, separated, both whites and yolks reserved

Kosher salt

Crusty bread, for serving

HEAT THE OLIVE OIL, garlic, and red pepper flakes in a large sauté pan that's 6 to 8 inches (15 to 30 cm) deep set over medium-low heat. Once the garlic starts to brown around the edges, 5 to 7 minutes, add the tomato sauce, Calabrian chile (if using), and the parsley, basil, and chives. Cook until the volume of the sauce is reduced by half, about 10 minutes.

Add the egg whites and stir them into the sauce using a chopstick or the handle of a wooden spoon. Spoon in the yolks, distributing them evenly around the pan, keeping each yolk intact. Keep on the heat for another minute and a half (or a little longer if you prefer your yolks more cooked). Serve immediately, either family-style from the pan or divided among individual plates with crusty bread on the side.

CHAPTER 3

Soups, Salads, *and* Antipasti

When I was growing up, appetizers consisted of huge platters of finger food—meats, cheeses, Fritto Misto (page 47), or fried squash blossoms (page 55) from my grandfather's garden—served on holidays and at family dinners that drew everyone to the table. It was a soulful, convivial way to start a meal: a little messy, a little rowdy, but always delicious and a lot of fun. Of course, later, when I was coming up as a chef, I developed a more refined approach to appetizers (check out the Chestnut Soup on page 44 and the Romaine Hearts with Dijon-Shallot Vinaigrette on page 59, both mainstays at Chianti), and learned to appreciate the grace of those clean, quieter flavors. But I'm still an antipasti guy at heart: To me, the welcoming and spirited character of those big platters is as powerful as the mix of flavors.

ANTIPASTO SALAD WITH OREGANO VINAIGRETTE

This kitchen sink–style salad is inspired by the huge platters of antipasti we would start every holiday meal off with when I was a kid. That abundant mixture of flavors and textures—from creamy cheese to salty meat to piquant peppers to crunchy vegetables—is re-created here in chopped-salad form, topped with an herby oregano vinaigrette. Don't be scared by the long list of ingredients: once all of the elements are prepared, the salad comes together in an instant. All the different tastes are key to getting that particular Italian-American family flavor—whenever I make this for lunch, my wife says she feels like she's in Brooklyn again.

Serves 6 to 8

½ cup (40 g) pimento-stuffed green olives, sliced crosswise into thirds

¼ cup (40 g) Gaeta olives or any black olives, pits removed, roughly chopped

6 sweet peppers, blistered over an open flame, skin removed, and cut into ¼-inch-thick slices

¼ cup (40 g) finely diced white or yellow onion

½ cup (75 g) cherry or grape tomatoes, cut into quarters

3 stalks celery, hearts cut into ¼-inch-thick slices, plus ½ cup (25 g) celery leaves

1 tablespoon chopped fresh flat-leaf parsley

¼ cup (30 g) sundried tomatoes in oil, drained and thinly sliced

½ teaspoon Calabrian chile

¼ cup (35 g) thinly sliced pickled pepperoncini peppers, plus ¼ cup brine from the jar

½ cup (100 g) Genoa salami, cut into ½-inch (12 mm) cubes

2½ ounces (70 g) provolone cheese, cut into ½-inch (12 mm) cubes

⅓ cup (75 ml) extra-virgin olive oil

¼ cup (60 ml) red wine vinegar

½ teaspoon dried oregano

1 teaspoon chopped fresh oregano leaves (optional)

3 heads butter lettuce, leaves separated

IN A LARGE MIXING BOWL, combine the olives, sweet peppers, onion, cherry tomatoes, sundried tomatoes, celery stalks, chile pepper, salami, and provolone and toss well.

In a separate bowl, whisk together the juice from the pepper jar, the olive oil, vinegar, dried oregano (and fresh oregano, if using). Toss the dressing with the antipasti. Set the antipasti aside at room temperature or place in the refrigerator to let the flavors marinate at least 20 minutes before serving.

When ready to serve, arrange the butter lettuce leaves on a platter and spoon the antipasti mixture on top, being careful not to break the lettuce. Sprinkle the celery leaves on the very top. The dressed antipasti mixture will keep in the refrigerator for a few days, but do not combine it with the lettuce until the very end, as the acid from the dressing will cause the leaves to wilt.

CHESTNUT SOUP

Chestnut soup—which was on Chianti's original menu—is a staple of the wintertime Italian table, but it isn't as common in the United States. That's a shame, because chestnuts have a wonderful, clean, distinctive flavor that really shines in a simple puréed soup. (Frozen chestnuts are available in most supermarkets; you can throw them directly into the hot saucepan straight from the package—no need to thaw them first!) That said, this is an extremely versatile recipe that I make all the time using whatever ingredients I have around—sunchokes, pumpkin, and butternut squash are some of my favorite variations. So if you want to switch up the chestnuts for another vegetable, go for it.

Note: I happen to like the depth that the truffle butter adds, but if you can't find it or prefer a lighter soup, it's okay to omit the truffle butter entirely.

Serves 6 to 8

⅓ cup plus ½ cup (75 ml plus 120 ml) extra-virgin olive oil

1 cup (110 g) diced onions

¼ teaspoon crushed red pepper

1 teaspoon kosher salt, plus more as needed

2 pounds frozen chestnuts

1 quart (660 ml) warm chicken or vegetable broth or stock, plus additional to thin soup as needed

2 teaspoons store-bought truffle butter (optional)

FOR THE GARNISH:

1 cup (130 g) frozen chestnuts, thawed and roughly chopped

2 tablespoons roughly chopped fresh flat-leaf parsley

Extra-virgin olive oil, for drizzling

IN A LARGE HEAVY-BOTTOMED POT on medium, heat ⅓ cup (75 ml) of the olive oil, the onions, red pepper flakes, and salt. Cook until the edges of the onions start to brown, 3 to 4 minutes.

Add the frozen chestnuts and the broth and simmer until the chestnuts are tender, 8 to 10 minutes.

Pour the contents of the pot into a blender with the remaining ½ cup (120 ml) olive oil and the truffle butter, if using. Blend until completely smooth and the soup has a nice sheen from the olive oil. (Or purée the soup in the pot using an immersion blender.) If the soup is too thick to pour in a smooth, steady stream, add more broth to thin, then adjust the seasoning with salt to taste.

Divide the soup among six soup bowls or eight cups and add some chopped chestnuts to each bowl. Sprinkle each serving with the parsley, add a drizzle of extra-virgin olive oil, and serve immediately.

FRITTO MISTO

Some foods are made for gathering, like a big platter of fritto misto, or a "mixed fry" of seafood and vegetables that is set on the table to share before a meal. This ingredient list provides a good baseline, though the beauty of fritto misto is that you can fry pretty much anything you like, in pretty much any combination. Feel free to adjust the ratio of vegetables to seafood, add or substitute other ingredients based on your taste and what is readily available, and increase the quantity for however many people you want to serve. The only constant is that this becomes a dish that fosters conviviality, something that entices people to linger around the table, telling stories, laughing, and enjoying each other's company, with a delicious bite always within reach.

Note: You really do need that much flour for dredging; otherwise it will get pasty. But you can sift together the flours and reserve them for the next time you make this.

Serves 6 to 8 as an appetizer

6 cups double zero (00) flour

2 cups rice flour

Kosher salt and black pepper

1 quart (960 ml) milk

6 green onions, light and dark green parts removed, cut from base 2½ inches (6 cm) long, root on, split in half

½ pound (225 g) cauliflower, stems and florets intact, cut into ¼-inch-thick slices

⅓ cup (30 g) julienned eggplant

6 Shishito peppers, split in half lengthwise

2 cups calamari, cut into strips

12 white anchovy fillets, cut lengthwise

2 quarts vegetable oil, or enough to submerge ingredients when frying

1 lemon, sliced into 8 thin wheels

3 tablespoons fresh rosemary leaves

20 leaves fresh flat-leaf parsley

9 leaves fresh sage

Pinch crushed red pepper, or to taste (optional)

10 Garlic Chips (page 27)

Lemon Aioli (recipe follows) and lemon wedges, for serving

Special equipment: a kitchen thermometer or an infrared thermometer

MIX TOGETHER THE FLOURS in a large bowl, season with salt and pepper, and set aside. Pour the milk into a separate large bowl, then add the green onions, cauliflower, eggplant, peppers, calamari, and anchovies and let them soak for at least 5 minutes, or up to 3 hours.

Drain the vegetables and seafood and dredge them in the seasoned flour mixture until all sides are well coated. Shake off excess flour and place them on a cookie sheet.

Pour the vegetable oil into a large pot and heat the oil until it reaches 365°F (185°C) on a kitchen thermometer or infrared thermometer. Carefully place the dredged vegetables and seafood in the pot and fry each piece until golden.

When the misto is just finished frying, add the lemon wheels to the hot oil and fry until crisp, about 2 to 4 minutes. Remove everything from the oil with tongs and drain on a clean towel. Transfer the fritto misto to a serving platter and season with salt, rosemary, parsley sage, and crushed red pepper, if using. Top with the garlic chips and serve immediately with lemon aioli and lemon wedges on the side.

Recipe continues

Lemon Aioli

Makes 1 cup (240 ml)

1 clove garlic

½ teaspoon kosher salt

1 cup (240 ml) mayonnaise

Zest and juice of 1 lemon

1 teaspoon finely chopped fresh flat-leaf parsley

Smash the garlic with the salt on a cutting board using the side of a large, heavy knife (or mash with a mortar and pestle). Continue to crush the salt into the garlic until it becomes a paste.

Combine the garlic paste mayonnaise, lemon zest and juice, and parsley in a bowl and whisk to combine. Cover and refrigerate until ready to use. (The aioli will last for up to a few days in an airtight container.)

KATHY'S SPINACH SOUP AND CHICKEN MEATBALLS

Our neighbor Kathy Vitone was a fixture of my childhood, as prominent a figure in my early life as my own parents. Every night after dinner, she would come over to our house with a glass of iced tea to decompress and talk to my mom. She also doted on me and my siblings; Kathy often called my mom to say, "Hey, can I take Scotty today?" And so I spent countless hours hanging out with her, watching TV together, playing, talking, and, of course, eating. She was a fantastic cook—in addition to this soup, she made a killer red pepper relish—and a warm and compassionate person who later got me my first cooking job at a local restaurant called the Sea Loft, which her husband owned. She was a huge influence on my life and my career, and this soup, which she often made for lunch on those days that we spent together, is an homage to that friendship.

Prep Note: The panko-and-milk mixture needs to rest for 2 hours before you can make the meatballs.

Serves 6 to 8

The Meatballs

¾ cup (60 g) panko

¾ cup (180 ml) milk

10 ounces (280 g) ground chicken

1½ tablespoons grated Parmigiano-Reggiano cheese

1½ tablespoons ricotta cheese

1 tablespoon chopped fresh parsley

1½ teaspoons chopped fresh rosemary

2 teaspoons kosher salt

Pinch crushed red pepper

1 large egg

Combine the panko and milk in a bowl and let it sit for 2 hours at room temperature, then lightly press out excess milk and discard the soaking liquid.

Put the milk-soaked panko in the bowl of a stand mixer fitted with a paddle attachment. Add the ground chicken, Parmigiano, ricotta, parsley, rosemary, salt, red pepper flakes, and egg and mix at low speed until the ingredients are just combined. (Do not overmix or the fat in the chicken will start to separate from the protein.) Cover and place it in the refrigerator overnight.

Line a cookie sheet with parchment paper. Roll out the meatballs to the size of a black olive on the parchment paper and chill in the refrigerator until the meatballs are cold throughout, about 1 hour. (You should have about 32 meatballs.)

Recipe continues

The Soup

3 to 4 tablespoons (45 to 60 ml) extra-virgin olive oil

4 cups (440 g) diced yellow onions (from about 2 medium onions)

2 to 3 teaspoons kosher salt, plus more as desired

3 to 4 cloves garlic, minced

2 quarts/liters chicken stock or broth

1 recipe Meatballs (page 49)

3 bunches spinach

FOR THE GARNISH:

¼ cup (25 g) grated Parmigiano-Reggiano cheese

2 tablespoons chopped fresh flat-leaf parsley

In a large heavy-bottomed pot, heat the olive oil on medium heat. Sweat the onions with 2 teaspoons of salt in the olive oil for 2 to 3 minutes, or until the onions are translucent.

Add the minced garlic and continue to cook for about 2 minutes, stirring with a wooden spoon to make sure the garlic does not burn.

Pour in the chicken broth, raise the heat to medium-high, and bring the soup to a boil, then carefully drop in the meatballs, and bring the heat back up to a boil. Reduce the heat to a simmer and cook, uncovered, until the meatballs are cooked through, about 10 minutes. Taste and add an additional teaspoon of salt (or more), if desired.

Stir in the spinach and cook it until just wilted. Remove the pot from heat. Serve the soup immediately, topping each bowl with chopped parsley and some grated Parmigiano-Reggiano.

PASTA E FAGIOLI

I love a soup that has a lot going on, ingredient-wise, then harmonizes flavor-wise when cooked. Pasta e fagioli, the staple of Italian (and many Italian-American) winter tables is just such a soup, and one that offers the additional bonus of being a completely satisfying one-pot meal. (The only other thing you need is some crusty bread to sop up the delicious bean broth.) It's also one of those dishes that improves as the flavors mingle, so it's a great thing to make ahead, or have on hand as leftovers. One thing to note: You need enough olive oil to really coat the starches of the beans, so don't be shy about adding more than is called for here if the beans look dry or pale while cooking; add enough to give them a nice sheen. This will make the beans more palatable and less grainy.

Serves 4 to 6

Prep Note: The beans require a combined cooking time of 1½ to 2 hours, so this dish is best to make when you aren't pressed for time.

1 cup (185 g) dried cannellini beans

1 cup (195 g) dried borlotti (cranberry) beans

¼ cup (60 ml) extra-virgin olive oil, plus more for serving

4 cups (110 g) chopped yellow or white onions (2 to 3 medium onions)

1½ teaspoons finely chopped fresh thyme

½ teaspoon crushed red pepper

1 tablespoon finely chopped garlic

1½ teaspoons finely chopped fresh oregano

2 sprigs rosemary

Kosher salt

8 ounces (225 g) prosciutto ends, skinned and cut into ¼-inch dice (optional)

1 (15-ounce/430 g) can puréed tomatoes

2 quarts/liters vegetable or chicken stock

2 cups (225 g) dried tubettini pasta

Grated Parmigiano-Reggiano cheese, for serving

Roughly chopped fresh flat-leaf parsley, for garnish

SOAK THE TWO TYPES OF BEANS in separate containers overnight in 4 cups (960 ml) water per container.

The next day, set the container of borlotti beans aside. Drain the water from the cannellini beans and place them in a pot. Add water to cover, bring to a simmer, and cook until tender, 1 to 1½ hours. Drain the cooked cannellini beans and set aside.

In a large pot, heat the olive oil over medium-high heat. Sweat the onions with the thyme, crushed red pepper, garlic, oregano, rosemary, and a little bit of salt to help release acid from the vegetables, 5 to 6 minutes. Continue to cook until the onions start to caramelize, 8 to 9 minutes. Add the prosciutto, if using, and cook for another minute. Add the tomatoes and cook for another minute, stirring to prevent the vegetables from burning. Pour in the stock, bring to a boil, then reduce the heat to a simmer. Drain the soaked borlotti beans, add them to the pot, and continue to simmer the broth until the beans are tender, about 1 hour.

While the beans are cooking, cook the pasta in heavily salted water until tender. Drain the pasta, without rinsing, reserving the pasta water. Toss the pasta with a little olive oil to prevent sticking, and set aside.

When the borlotti beans are tender, add the cannellini beans and return to a simmer. Add half the pasta cooking water, return to a simmer, and cook for at least 40 minutes.

Allow the soup to cool slightly, then remove one-fourth of the beans from the pot and set aside. Using a slotted spoon transfer the rest of the cooked beans to a blender and purée until smooth. (Or purée the soup in the pot using an immersion blender.)

Combine the tubettini and reserved beans and divide among four or six bowls. Pour the soup over the pasta and beans and serve immediately, topped with chopped parsley, grated Parmigiano-Reggiano, and a drizzle of olive oil. (The beans and soup can also be prepared the day before, refrigerated, and reheated, but you may need to add some additional stock, as the beans will absorb a lot of liquid as they sit. Do not add in the pasta before storing.)

ZUCCHINI BLOSSOMS, TWO WAYS

Each spring during my childhood, my grandfather and my uncle would regularly drive over garbage bags full of zucchini blossoms from their garden, which my mom would fry up and serve in piles that we'd eat like popcorn, shoveling them into our mouths. A more refined way of preparing them is stuffed with ricotta, roasted, and served over a delicate cherry tomato sauce. Which one is better really depends on the mood—do you want soulful and satisfying or elegantly composed? But you can't go wrong; both are delicious.

Fried Zucchini Blossoms

Serves 6 to 8

30 zucchini blossoms

6 large eggs

¼ cup (60 ml) milk, plus additional to thin out the batter, as needed

¾ teaspoon baking powder

1 teaspoon kosher salt, plus more for the fried blossoms

1 cup (125 g) plus 2 tablespoons all-purpose flour

1 tablespoon finely chopped fresh basil

1 cup (240 ml) vegetable oil, for frying

Clean the flowers by lightly rubbing them with a damp paper towel. (Do not wash them or they will turn to mush.) Set aside.

Beat the eggs with a whisk or in an electric mixer until frothy, 2 to 3 minutes, then set aside. Pour the milk into a large bowl, sift the baking powder, salt, and flour into the milk, then stir to make a thick batter. Gently fold in the beaten eggs along with the basil. (The batter should be a bit lighter and thinner than pancake batter.)

Heat the vegetable oil in a large skillet over medium-high heat; when hot, drop a few small drops of batter into the oil to test if it is hot enough for frying. (If the oil bubbles around the batter and it floats instantly, the oil's ready.)

Working in batches, dip each blossom into the batter to coat, then fry in the hot oil, about 1 to 2 minutes on each side, until the blossoms are golden brown. Remove the blossoms from the pan and place on paper towel–lined baking sheets to absorb the excess oil. Sprinkle the fried blossoms with salt, and repeat the process until all the blossoms are cooked. (You may need to thin the batter with milk as you go to maintain the correct consistency; when the starch absorbs the milk, it expands.)

Once all the blossoms are fried and drained, place them on a platter and serve immediately.

Recipe continues

Stuffed Zucchini Blossoms

Serves 6

12 zucchini blossoms

Extra-virgin olive oil, for greasing the baking sheet

2 cups (490 g) ricotta cheese

¼ teaspoon kosher salt, plus more for the fried blossoms

¼ teaspoon ground black pepper

1 large egg yolk

1 teaspoon chopped anchovy in its oil

Pinch crushed red pepper

¼ tablespoon chopped fresh oregano

2 tablespoons grated Parmigiano-Reggiano cheese

FOR THE TOMATO SAUCE:

1 tablespoon extra-virgin olive oil

1½ teaspoons thinly sliced garlic

1 pint (290 g) mixed tomatoes, cut in half

1½ teaspoons chopped basil leaves

Preheat the oven to 325°F (165°C).

Clean the flowers by lightly rubbing them with a damp paper towel. (Do not wash them or they will turn to mush.) Set aside.

Lightly coat a baking sheet with oil. Mix together the ricotta, salt, pepper, egg yolk, anchovy in oil, crushed red pepper, and oregano until well combined. Transfer the ricotta mixture to a piping bag. (If you do not have a piping bag, you can use a ziptight bag and cut off one corner.) Pipe about 1 tablespoon filling into each blossom and place them on the prepared baking sheet. Sprinkle the Parmigiano-Reggiano on the blossoms and bake for 9 minutes.

While the blossoms are baking, make the tomato sauce: In a sauté pan over medium-high, heat the olive oil slightly. Add the garlic slices and sauté for 30 seconds. (Do not let garlic take on any color.) Add the cherry tomatoes and a pinch of salt and continue to sauté until the tomatoes have released their juice and the juice has been cooked off, about 8 minutes. Add the basil and mix to incorporate. The sauce should be chunky and fresh looking.

Spread the tomato sauce on a platter and arrange the baked blossoms on top. Serve immediately.

PICKLED EGGPLANT

It's hard to choose, but if you twist my arm, I'd say this is probably my all-time favorite anti-pasto. It's a very traditional southern Italian preparation, and something I grew up eating not just before meals, but at pretty much all hours of the day. (One of my favorite breakfasts was a big scoop of this on a piece of bread that my siblings and I would eat on the way to school, olive oil dripping all over our clothes.) Today, I like to serve it with burrata because I love the way the sharpness of the pickled eggplant plays off of the creaminess of the cheese. It does take a full three days of salting, soaking, and marinating the eggplant to really get the flavors in sync, but trust me—it's worth the wait. And don't skimp on the olive oil: That rich, unctuous layer of flavored oil at the bottom of the bowl is heaven, and well worth whatever cleaning has to be done to your clothes afterward.

Prep Note: This dish requires 3 overnight soaks before it is ready to serve.

Makes 1 pint (480 ml)

1½ pounds eggplant (about 2 to 3 large eggplants), peeled, cut crosswise into ¼-inch-thick slices, and julienned

2 tablespoons kosher salt

White wine vinegar, enough to cover the eggplant

1½ teaspoons chopped fresh oregano

1 clove garlic, smashed

½ teaspoon crushed red pepper

1½ cups (360 ml) extra-virgin olive oil

IN A NONREACTIVE CONTAINER, toss the eggplant with the salt and let sit overnight in the refrigerator.

The next day, tightly squeeze the eggplant to drain out excess water. Reserve the eggplant and discard the salted liquid. Rinse the container, then add the eggplant and enough white wine vinegar to completely cover it. Place a lid on the container, and soak overnight in the refrigerator.

The next day, remove the eggplant from the vinegar, lightly squeeze, then put the eggplant in a mixing bowl with the oregano, smashed garlic clove, and crushed red pepper. Add enough oil to completely cover the eggplant, cover the container with a lid or plastic wrap, and let sit for at least overnight in the refrigerator before serving. If there are any leftovers, the pickled eggplant can be stored in a glass jar for up to a month.

ROMAINE HEARTS WITH DIJON-SHALLOT VINAIGRETTE

The dressing on this salad was Chianti's house dressing and it was very popular. (Though we kept a special honey-spiked stash in the kitchen for one of our favorite regulars, a neighborhood guy we called "Nice Guy" Eddie, who preferred things on the sweeter side.) This is also essentially the house dressing of my own home—I always have a bottle of it in the fridge ready to go. The combination of olive and grapeseed oils gives this vinaigrette a subtle complexity you don't want to miss, so it's best on a simple salad of lettuce and croutons, punctuated only by the acid kick of pickled onions.

Serves 6

6 to 8 romaine hearts

¾ cup (180 ml) Dijon-Shallot Vinaigrette (recipe follows)

1 cup (235 g) Pickled Red Onions (recipe follows)

1 cup (55 g) Ciabatta Croutons (recipe follows)

1¾ ounces (50 g) Parmigiano-Reggiano cheese

Kosher salt and freshly cracked black pepper

CUT THE ROOT ENDS OFF the hearts of romaine to loosen the leaves. Wash and pat them dry using paper towels. Tear the leaves in half lengthwise by hand.

Place the romaine in a serving bowl, then drizzle the dressing over the top. Scatter the pickled onions and croutons over the top. Shave the Parmigiano-Reggiano over the top. (You can use a vegetable peeler to shave the cheese if you don't have a cheese shaver.) Season with salt and freshly cracked pepper and serve immediately.

Dijon-Shallot Vinaigrette

Makes ¾ cup (180 ml)

2 tablespoons apple cider vinegar

1 tablespoon red wine vinegar

2 tablespoons lemon juice

¼ cup (60 ml) extra-virgin olive oil

¼ cup (60 ml) grapeseed oil

1 teaspoon Dijon mustard

1 small shallot, peeled and halved

Pinch kosher salt

Dash Worcestershire sauce

Place all the ingredients in a blender and blend until smooth. The dressing can be served immediately, or will hold in the refrigerator up to 1 week.

Recipe continues

Pickled Red Onions

Makes 1 cup (235 g)

½ cup (120 ml) red wine vinegar

1 teaspoon kosher salt

1 cup (110 g) thinly sliced red onion

Combine the vinegar and salt in a saucepan and bring to a simmer. Put the onions in a glass jar and pour the vinegar over them. Cover and refrigerate for at least 1 day before using. The pickled onions will hold for several weeks in the refrigerator.

Ciabatta Croutons

Makes 1 cup (55 g)

Prep Note: These are "fresh" croutons, which are still soft in the middle, so it is not recommended that you make them ahead of time.

1 cup (45 g) bite-sized cubes of ciabatta (tear them by hand)

3 tablespoons extra-virgin olive oil

Kosher salt and freshly cracked black pepper

Put the ciabatta in a bowl and toss with the olive oil and salt and pepper to taste.

Toast the seasoned bread cubes in a dry sauté pan over low heat, tossing continually so they do not burn. When the edges of the cubes are golden brown and crunchy, take them off the heat and reserve until ready to use.

CHAPTER 4

Pasta, Baby

When I came to New York, I fell in love with the city, and I fell in love with making pasta. I was no stranger to eating pasta, of course, but the pasta I had eaten at home growing up was, I came to realize, a completely different category of pasta: rustic, soulful, always satisfying, but not exacting. Preparing it was something you did, not something you thought about. The kitchens I worked in when I first came to New York changed all of that.

At San Domenico, where I held my first restaurant position in New York, I was exposed to a level of finesse and artfulness in the preparation of pasta that had, quite frankly, never occurred to me before. It wasn't pretentious; on the contrary, the thoughtfulness and precision of the chefs I worked under amplified pasta's inherent and beautiful simplicity. They didn't overdo it with luxury ingredients but honored this universal category of food by instead taking into account its every nuance: how each type of pasta, particular shape, and dough composition should inform what it is prepared with. This approach resonated with me immediately, and I studied their every move. Eventually I became the first American to head up the pasta station there, and pasta became (and remains) the category of food that is closest to my heart, even (or especially) now that I've come full circle and returned to cooking it regularly at home for my own family.

PASTA POMODORO

Without further ado: my greatest hit, the dish I'm asked to trot out everywhere I go. What makes my version of the most classic Italian pasta preparation so crave-able is, I think, that it's the sum of a lot of parts treated with respect: the truly fresh tomatoes, the unhurried 45-minute cook time, and the inclusion of butter, which rounds out the acidity of the tomatoes and olive oil in the finish. (Finishing pasta with a touch of butter is a trick from restaurant kitchens that's easy to do at home and adds depth to the overall flavor of the dish.) No single detail is the secret weapon per se—and nothing about this recipe is hard to do—but the key is not cutting any corners, because in a dish this straightforward, every nuance counts.

Note: The sauce recipe makes double what you'll need for the finished dish, but I do not recommend cutting it down because you need that volume of ingredients to get the flavor right. There are lots of other uses for this sauce in the book, including Eggs in Purgatory (page 39), Eggplant Caponata (page 16), and as a base for the Spinach and Ricotta Gnudi and the Pork Ragù in this chapter (pages 71 and 82).

Serves 6

POMODORO SAUCE :

Makes about 2 quarts/liters

5 pounds (2.3 kg) ripe plum or Roma tomatoes

1½ teaspoons kosher salt, plus more to taste

4 cloves garlic, peeled

¼ cup (60 ml) extra-virgin olive oil

1 teaspoon crushed red pepper

1 cup (40 g) loosely packed fresh basil leaves

PREPARE A POT OF BOILING WATER and an ice bath. Core the tomatoes, cut a small x on the bottom, then blanch the tomatoes in the boiling water for 1 minute and, using a slotted spoon or a spider, transfer them to the ice bath. When cool enough to handle, remove the skins with a paring knife and discard them. Slice the tomatoes in half and strain through a fine-mesh sieve set over a bowl. Discard the seeds but reserve the liquid. Combine the deseeded, peeled tomatoes, reserved juice, and salt in a large bowl. Mix the salt into the tomatoes and set aside.

Place the garlic in a saucepan, cover with the olive oil, and cook over very low heat until the garlic is golden and soft, about 20 minutes. (Watch it carefully, and shake the pan occasionally to make sure the garlic doesn't burn.) Strain and reserve the garlic-infused oil. (Save the garlic cloves for another use, such as the roasted garlic spread on page 18.)

In a large heavy-bottomed stockpot, cook the red pepper flakes in the infused garlic oil over low heat for about 2 minutes, until the red pepper flakes become fragrant and the flavor starts to bloom. Add the salted tomatoes and tomato liquid to the pot and raise the heat to medium-high. Bring the liquid to a slight boil and skim off the foam that rises to the top. Reduce the heat to medium low, and then, using a potato masher, mash the tomatoes very finely as they cook. Simmer until the sauce is reduced by one-fourth, about 25 to 30 minutes, then taste and adjust the seasoning with salt.

Remove from heat and stir in the basil. Prepare with pasta according to the directions on page 66, or cover and store until ready to use. (The sauce can be kept in the refrigerator in an airtight container for up to a week, or in the freezer for about 1 month. Cool the sauce to room temperature before storing it.)

Recipe continues

FOR SERVING:

Kosher salt

1 recipe Fresh Spaghetti (page 97)

½ recipe Pomodoro Sauce (about 1 quart/960 ml; see page 64)

Crushed red pepper

¾ cup (1½ sticks/115 g) unsalted butter

¾ cup (70 g) grated Parmigiano-Reggiano cheese, plus additional for garnish

Extra-virgin olive oil

12 sliced fresh basil leaves

Bring a pot of heavily salted water to a boil. (The water should have the salinity of broth.)

Meanwhile, in a sauté pan over medium-high heat, reduce the Pomodoro sauce by about one-fourth, then season with crushed red pepper and salt; keep warm while you cook the pasta.

When the water boils, add the pasta and cook until just shy of al dente (about 75 percent done), 4 to 5 minutes. Remove ½ cup (120 ml) pasta cooking liquid, then drain the pasta. (Do not rinse.) Add the pasta and a few table-spoons of the cooking water to the sauté pan to finish cooking the pasta with the sauce, adding additional cooking water as needed. Remove from heat, then add the butter, cheese, olive oil to taste, and the basil leaves. Toss to combine, so that the butter and olive oil emulsify in the tomato sauce. Serve immediately, with additional grated Parmigiano-Reggiano on top.

SPAGHETTI AGLIO E OLIO WITH ANCHOVIES

If I had to pick one pasta to eat forever, this is it. When it's done properly, the purity of the flavors is something really special. It doesn't even truly have a sauce: The pasta is just lightly coated with garlic and anchovies, which are bound to it by the emulsified oil and starchy pasta-cooking water. This is a real, traditional pull-it-out-of-your-pantry type of dish, so I would even discourage you from substituting fresh pasta for the dried that is called for. My big tip: Use the biggest pan that you can find. You need a large surface area so that the starch that's released can really coat the pasta, which gives this dish its beautiful texture. Also, cheese is verboten: Despite the simplicity of its ingredients, this dish packs a ton of flavor. Don't let anything else get in the way.

Serves 4 to 6

Kosher salt

1 pound (455 g) dried spaghetti

½ cup (120 ml) extra-virgin olive oil

6 anchovy fillets, plus 1 tablespoon oil from the jar

6 large cloves garlic, thinly sliced

1 teaspoon crushed red pepper

¼ cup (13 g) roughly chopped fresh flat-leaf parsley

Toasted breadcrumbs (recipe follows)

BRING A POT OF HEAVILY SALTED WATER to a boil. (The water should have the salinity of broth.)

Add the pasta and start the timer.

While the pasta is cooking, heat the olive oil in a large sauté pan, then add the anchovies and anchovy oil, garlic cloves, and crushed red pepper and cook over medium heat, stirring to gently break up the bodies of the anchovies, until the edges of the garlic start to brown.

When the spaghetti is just shy of al dente (about 75 percent of the total cook time recommended on the package), remove ½ cup (120 ml) of the pasta cooking water, then drain the spaghetti. (Do not rinse.)

Add the drained pasta and a few tablespoons of the cooking water to the pan with the garlic and anchovies. Toss to make sure that the pasta gets completely coated, adding additional cooking water as needed, to create an emulsion of starch and oil. Remove from heat, add the parsley, toss, and season with salt to taste. Transfer to a serving dish or individual bowls, top with toasted breadcrumbs, and serve immediately.

Toasted Breadcrumbs

1 cup (80 g) panko

1 teaspoon crushed red pepper

¼ cup (60 ml) extra-virgin olive oil

Kosher salt

Combine the panko, crushed red pepper, olive oil, and salt to taste in a saucepan and sauté until golden brown, continuously stirring or tossing for 6 to 8 minutes. (Watch the pan carefully as you sauté so you can remove the breadcrumbs as soon as they are golden.)

Pasta, Baby

CAVATELLI WITH BRAISED DUCK RAGÙ AND BLACK TRUFFLES

If you like ragù, I recommend keeping this in your regular rotation; the flavors are complex and refined, but the dish itself is comforting and crowd-pleasing. The ragù also freezes well, so it's something I like to have on hand for weeknight meals—or prepare for Mel when I travel so she's got something easy to pull together when she's alone with the kids. The black truffles are optional, but worth it if you can get them. It's a great dish without them, but it's a better dish with them.

Serves 6

FOR THE RAGÙ:

Makes 1 quart (960 ml)

1½ pounds (680 g) duck legs

½ medium onion, sliced into half-moons

1 medium stalk celery, sliced crosswise

3 cups (720 ml) dry red wine

1 teaspoon whole black peppercorns

2 fresh bay leaves

2 to 3 whole cloves

Kosher salt

2 tablespoons truffle juice, from canned black truffles (optional; the truffles will be served with the finished dish)

2 sprigs fresh rosemary

1 tablespoon chopped sage

3 to 4 sprigs fresh thyme

3 to 4 cloves garlic

1 (15-ounce/430 g) can puréed tomatoes

1 tablespoon tomato paste

1 cup (240 ml) chicken stock

CLEAN THE DUCK LEGS and remove their skin. Finely chop the onion and celery in a food processor. Combine the red wine, onion and celery, peppercorns, bay leaves, and cloves in a nonreactive airtight container. Add the duck legs and let them soak for 12 hours or overnight.

Remove the legs from the marinade and strain the vegetables and spices from the wine, reserving both.

Season both sides of the duck legs with salt and sear them in a large heavy-bottomed pot over medium-high heat until a nice deep golden color develops on both sides. Remove most of the duck fat from the pan, but do not clean it.

Add the reserved vegetables and the truffle liquid to the pot that the duck was seared in and cook over medium heat for 25 to 30 minutes to draw out moisture. Lower the heat to medium-low and continue to cook for another 30 minutes. Once the vegetables are caramelized, add the rosemary, sage, thyme, and garlic, and then return the seared legs to the pan along with the tomato paste and mix to combine. Add the reserved marinade, the puréed tomatoes, and the chicken stock, making sure the duck legs are covered. Turn up the heat to high, bring to a boil, then reduce heat and simmer for 1 hour, until the duck legs are tender and the liquid has reduced by half. There should be enough braising liquid to just cover the legs; if you have a lot more than that, continue to reduce. Remove the legs from the braising liquid and let them cool.

Remove the meat from the bones, then return the meat to the cooking liquid and let the ragù chill in the fridge overnight, or until you're ready to cook the pasta. (Skim the duck fat from the sauce once it has cooled completely.)

Recipe continues

FOR SERVING:

Kosher salt

1 recipe Cavatelli (page 94)

1 recipe Duck Ragù (1 quart) (see previous page)

2 tablespoons canned black truffles, chopped (optional)

3 tablespoons unsalted butter

¼ cup (25 g) grated Parmigiano-Reggiano cheese

¼ cup (60 ml) extra-virgin olive oil

3 tablespoons chopped fresh chives

Bring a big pot of heavily salted water to a boil. (The water should have the salinity of broth.)

While the water is boiling, place the ragù in a saucepan large enough to contain the pasta, too, and begin to warm the sauce. When the water boils, add the cavatelli and cook until it is just shy of al dente (about 75 percent done), 4 to 6 minutes. Remove ½ cup (120 ml) of the pasta cooking water, then drain the cavatelli. (Do not rinse.) Add the pasta and about half of the reserved cooking water to the pan with the ragù and cook for 2 minutes, adding more of the pasta cooking water as you go if the ragù looks dry. Stir in the truffles, remove from heat, then stir in the butter, cheese, olive oil, and chives. Serve immediately.

SPINACH AND RICOTTA GNUDI WITH CONCENTRATED TOMATO SAUCE AND CRISPY GUANCIALE

Let's not beat around the bush: If you do it right, this is the sexiest dish in the book. It does require a bit of prep to nail the texture of each component, but the bright, clear contrasts of the bite of the pasta against the ooziness of the cheese, and the richness of the beurre monté against the assertiveness of the tomato sauce are irresistible. That concentrated tomato sauce (a classic pomodoro base—on page 64—enhanced with *estratto*, or high-quality extracted tomato paste) is the secret weapon: You don't need much of this tomato paste, and if you've never cooked with it, you'll be amazed at how the *estratto* thickens the sauce by absorbing liquid, resulting in a thick, hyper-flavorful concentrate that's almost like a roux. The gnudi doesn't really need anything else, though if you want to guild the lily, add the crispy guanciale for crunch and umami.

Serves 6

Kosher salt

1 recipe Gnudi (page 96)

1 recipe Beurre Monté (recipe follows)

¾ cup (180 ml) Concentrated Tomato Sauce (recipe follows)

1 recipe Fried Guanciale (optional; recipe follows)

2 tablespoons finely chopped chives

12 small fresh basil leaves

BRING A POT OF HEAVILY SALTED WATER to a boil. (The water should be the salinity of broth.)

Meanwhile, in a large sauté pan set over low heat, add the beurre monté and begin to warm it. When the water boils, add the gnudi to the pot. Once they float to the top of the water, allow them to cook for another 30 seconds, then use a spider or slotted spoon to remove the gnudi and add them to the pan with the beurre monté. Cook until completely warmed through, about 1½ minutes.

Remove from heat and place the contents of the pan in a large serving bowl. Add dollops of the concentrated tomato sauce and the crispy guanciale (if using) on top. Sprinkle with the chives and basil leaves and serve immediately.

Recipe continues

CONCENTRATED TOMATO SAUCE:

Makes about 1 cup (120 ml)

1 cup (240 ml) Pomodoro Sauce (page 64)

1 teaspoon estratto di pomodoro or another high-quality tomato paste

2 tablespoons extra-virgin olive oil

Pinch crushed red pepper

In a large sauté pan, warm the pomodoro sauce over medium-low heat. Put the estratto in a saucepan and cut up the tomato paste with the back of a spoon. Add the olive oil and red pepper to the tomato paste and stir to combine. Add the warm pomodoro sauce and continue cooking, whisking occasionally, until the sauce is a uniform color and texture, about 5 minutes. Remove from heat and set aside until you're ready to prepare the gnudi.

Beurre Monté

Makes about ½ cup (120 ml)

½ cup (120 ml) heavy cream

1 sprig thyme

1½ teaspoons cornstarch

1 cup (2 sticks/225 g) unsalted butter, diced

Pinch kosher salt

In a heavy-bottomed pot over medium-high heat, bring the heavy cream with the sprig of thyme to a simmer.

Whisk the cornstarch and 1½ tablespoons water together to make a slurry and stir it into the heavy cream. Once the cream has thickened, remove the thyme sprig and discard.

Reduce heat to low, then gradually whisk in the diced butter into the cream to create a nice sauce-like consistency. Season with a pinch of salt and keep warm until ready to use.

Crispy Guanciale

6 ounces (170 g) guanciale, very thinly sliced (you can ask your butcher to slice it)

Preheat the oven to 350°F (175°C). Lay the guanciale slices on a baking sheet lined with a silicone baking mat. Cover with another silicone mat and weigh down the cured pork with additional baking sheets.

Bake in the preheated oven until the guanciale is golden brown and crispy—check the texture every 5 minutes; it should take about 15 minutes total. Remove from the oven, lift off the baking sheets and baking mat, and move the guanciale to paper towels to drain. Serve immediately.

MACCHERONI WITH POLPETTINE AND NEAPOLITAN TOMATO SAUCE

This is spaghetti and meatballs, Italian style. *Polpettine* ("little meatballs") are less common in America, but I have long been a big fan, because you get the complete meatball flavor in each bite. The tomato sauce is different too: instead of being bright and fresh like the Pomodoro Sauce on page 64, it is cooked down, so it's heartier and more savory. Maccheroni is similar to spaghetti but thicker, which allows it to stand up to the bold flavors of the sauce and meatballs. (I like to cut mine shorter than spaghetti as well, so each strand is about 4 to 6 inches [10 to 15 cm] long.) All together, this is a no-nonsense, fully satisfying plate of pasta—or as I like to think of it, a real "nonna dish."

Serves 6

NEAPOLITAN TOMATO SAUCE:

Makes 5 to 6 cups (1.2 to 1.4 liters)

8 ounces (225 g) beef chuck, cut in 2-inch (5 cm) pieces

½ medium white onion, sliced into half-moons

1 clove garlic, thinly sliced

2 celery stalks, sliced

1 teaspoon crushed red pepper

1 tablespoon dried oregano

10 plum or Roma tomatoes, quartered

1 (15-ounce/430 g) can puréed tomatoes

Kosher salt and freshly ground black pepper

5 fresh basil leaves

PUT THE CHUCK BEEF, onion, garlic, celery, crushed red pepper, and oregano in a large Dutch oven over medium heat, and roast uncovered until the meat is browned, 6 or 7 minutes. Add the plum tomatoes and cook for an additional 30 minutes, stirring occasionally so the sauce does not burn on the bottom of the pot. Add the canned tomatoes and salt and pepper to taste and cook for another hour, stirring occasionally. Stir in the basil and cook for an additional 5 minutes.

Remove from heat and purée the sauce using either a food mill or a food processor, and season with salt and pepper. Serve immediately, or store in the refrigerator until ready to use. (The sauce can hold in the refrigerator for about a week, or up to 1 month if frozen in an airtight container.)

Recipe continues

Polpettine

Makes about 120 meatballs

2 pounds (910 g) prime beef chuck, ground

2 tablespoons chopped fresh flat-leaf parsley

2 slices white bread, soaked in milk for 10 minutes, squeezed, and chopped (about ¾ cup)

⅓ cup (60 g) ricotta cheese

1 teaspoon chopped garlic

3 tablespoons grated Parmigiano-Reggiano cheese

1 teaspoon dried oregano

2 large eggs

Kosher salt and freshly ground black pepper

Put the ground chuck, parsley, soaked white bread, ricotta, garlic, Parmigiano, oregano, and eggs in a large bowl and mix well with a wooden spoon, or with your hands using food-safe gloves. Season with salt and pepper. (You can also test cook a small patty to taste for seasoning and adjust from that.)

Scoop out a small amount of meatball mixture and roll into small balls, about the size of the tip of your thumb. Store on parchment-lined baking sheets in the refrigerator until chilled all the way through (about 1 hour), then cook according to the directions at right.

FOR SERVING:

Kosher salt

1 recipe Maccheroni (page 97)

6 tablespoons (85 g) unsalted butter

6 tablespoons (90 ml) extra-virgin olive oil

1 recipe uncooked Polpettine (left)

1 recipe Neapolitan Tomato Sauce (page 73)

¾ cup (70 g) grated Parmigiano-Reggiano cheese

Freshly ground black pepper

Bring a large pot of heavily salted water to a boil. (The water should have the salinity of broth.)

While you wait for the water to boil, in a large pan, warm 3 tablespoons of the butter and 3 tablespoons of the oil, then add the polpettine in a single layer and sauté them until warmed through and browned. Spoon the polpettine into a separate 6- to 8-inch-deep pan (you can use the pan that the tomato sauce was cooked in, if large enough), add the sauce, and simmer for 5 minutes.

Add the pasta to the pan and cook until just shy of al dente (about 75 percent done), about 3 minutes. Remove and reserve at least 1 cup (240 ml) of the pasta cooking water, then drain the pasta. (Do not rinse it.)

Increase the heat under the sauce to medium-high, then add the pasta to the pan along with some of the pasta cooking water, a few tablespoons at a time. Stir to completely coat the pasta with the sauce; when you shake the pan, the sauce and pasta should move together.

Remove from heat, add the cheese, the remaining 3 tablespoons butter and 3 tablespoons olive oil, and toss until fully incorporated. Season with salt and pepper to taste and serve immediately.

FUSILLI WITH CHICKEN LIVERS AND NEONATA

It's shocking to me how much people love this dish—I never thought of chicken livers as being something that people crave, but whenever we've had this on the menu, people have gone crazy for it. As usual, the key is the interplay of the flavors: the iron content of the liver mixed with the sweetness of peas and the pungent spice of neonata. Neonata is a condiment from southern Italy, made from baby fish and peppers. (*Neonata* means "newborn" in Italian.) It isn't hard to find online, but you can substitute Calabrian chile and a little extra fish sauce if necessary.

Serves 6

2 teaspoons kosher salt, plus more for the pasta cooking water

1 pound (455 g) dried long fusilli pasta

3 cloves garlic, thinly sliced

¼ cup (60 ml) extra-virgin olive oil, plus additional for drizzling

Pinch crushed red pepper

1½ cups (190 g) finely diced onion

1¼ pounds (570 g) chicken livers, rinsed, dried, cleaned (blood veins and sinew removed), and roughly chopped

2 tablespoons unsalted butter

1 tablespoon fish sauce

2 tablespoons drained and chopped capers (not salt-packed)

2 tablespoons neonata (a spicy Italian fish sauce; see headnote)

2 cups (480 ml) passata or tomato purée

2 cups (270 g) frozen peas

⅓ cup (75 ml) extra-virgin olive oil

¼ cup (13 g) chopped fresh flat-leaf parsley

1 cup (100 g) grated Parmigiano-Reggiano cheese

BRING A LARGE POT OF HEAVILY SALTED WATER to a boil. (The water should have the salinity of broth.) Add the fusilli and cook according to package instructions.

While the pasta is cooking, in a large pot, cook the garlic, olive oil, crushed red pepper, and onions over medium heat. When the onions are translucent and just starting to get a little brown, 7 to 8 minutes, add the chicken livers and the salt and cook until the livers start to break apart, about 3 minutes, stirring well. Add the butter, fish sauce, capers, neonata, and the passata and cook until the sauce is slightly reduced, about 4 minutes.

When the pasta is al dente, drain, reserving at least 1 cup (240 ml) of the pasta cooking water. (Do not rinse the pasta.) Add the pasta and frozen peas to the sauce along with several tablespoons of pasta cooking water and cook for another 2 to 3 minutes, until the peas are warmed through, adding more pasta water if the sauce is too thick.

Remove from heat, drizzle a little olive oil over the top, and stir in the chopped parsley, and grated cheese. Serve immediately.

MALLOREDDUS WITH SAUSAGE AND PORCINI RAGÙ

Malloreddus is a small but mighty pasta from Sardinia, made from 100 percent semolina flour. Its shape resembles gnocchi (it is also known as *gnocchetti sardi*), but that's where the similarities end. Because of the semolina flour, malloreddus has a tough, almost resistant texture that can really stand up to a hearty ragù. (If you can't find malloreddus, *gemelli*, or a fresh extruded pasta, works as well.) The mingling among the textures of the pasta, the mushrooms, and the pieces of sausage is what I really love about this dish, although you could also omit the pasta, add a little more liquid to the ragù, and make it a soup.

Serves 6

SAUSAGE AND PORCINI RAGÙ:

Makes about 4 to 5 cups
(1 to 1.2 liters)

3 tablespoons dried porcini mushrooms

1½ cups (360 ml) hot water

6 tablespoons (90 ml) extra-virgin olive oil

12 ounces (340 g) sweet Italian sausage

1½ cups (190 g) finely diced onion

2 dried bay leaves

5 cloves garlic, chopped

¾ cup (180 ml) canned puréed tomatoes

1½ cups (360 ml) More than Gourmet roasted chicken stock or other brown chicken stock (see Special Ingredients on page 23)

Kosher salt

1 teaspoon crushed red pepper

SOAK THE DRIED PORCINI in the hot water until soft, about 10 minutes. Remove the rehydrated mushrooms from the water, reserving the liquid, and finely chop them.

In a sauté pan, heat the olive oil over medium heat. Remove the sausage from the casing, add it to the pan, and cook, using a wooden spoon to gently break apart the sausage into bite-sized pieces. Once the sausage is browned, 7 to 10 minutes, remove it from the pan and set aside.

Add the onion and bay leaves to the pan the sausages were browned in and sweat the onions over medium heat until soft, about 3 minutes, then add the garlic and continue to sweat until the garlic is soft as well, about 2 minutes. Add the mushrooms and cook for 10 minutes, or until their liquid has evaporated. Add the browned sausage, canned tomatoes, reserved porcini liquid, and brown chicken stock to the pan, reduce the heat, and simmer for 30 minutes.

Season the sauce with salt to taste and the crushed red pepper and prepare with the pasta, as described below, or cover and store until ready to use. (The ragù will last for up to 1 week in the refrigerator or it can be frozen for up to 1 month.)

Recipe continues

FOR SERVING

Kosher salt

1 pound (455 g) dried malloreddus pasta

1 recipe Sausage and Porcini Ragù (see previous page)

¾ cup (70 g) grated Parmigiano-Reggiano cheese

3 tablespoons unsalted butter

6 tablespoons (90 ml) extra-virgin olive oil

1 recipe Togarashi-Inspired Sunflower Spice
(optional; page 27)

Bring a pot of heavily salted water to a boil. (The water should have the salinity of broth.) Add the pasta.

While the pasta is cooking, place the ragù in a large sauté pan and begin to warm it over medium heat. When the pasta is just shy of al dente (about 75 percent of the total cook time listed on the package), remove about 1 cup (240 ml) of the pasta cooking water, then drain the pasta. (Do not rinse.) Add the pasta to the sauté pan along with a few tablespoons of pasta cooking water and stir to coat the pasta with the sauce, adding additional pasta water as needed. When the pasta is finished cooking, shake the pan—the sauce and pasta should move together.

Remove from heat, add the cheese, butter, and olive oil, and toss until well incorporated. Adjust the seasoning with salt, place in a large serving bowl, and top with the togarashi-inspired sunflower spice, if using. Serve immediately.

PICI WITH LOBSTER AND TARRAGON

Lobster is a big commitment—it's a lot of work, and it isn't cheap. This is a lobster dish that I think is worth the effort and expense. Pici is a pasta that's similar in shape to maccheroni (see page 97), but with tapered ends and a softer texture. It's commonly found in Tuscany, where it's typically served with meat sauces or cacio e pepe). The combination of pici with lobster meat, lobster stock, and tarragon is an invention of my own.

Serves 6

Lobster Stock

Makes 1 quart (960 ml)

2 medium onions, thinly sliced

1 head garlic

5 lobster heads, cleaned

1 cup (240 g) canned crushed tomatoes

4 sprigs thyme

4 sprigs oregano

½ cup (120 ml) chicken stock

In a large stockpot, sweat the onions and garlic over medium-high heat, 4 to 6 minutes, and then add the lobster heads, reducing the heat if the onions and garlic start to brown. Slowly roast the heads in the pot, and as they take on color, break up the shells with a potato masher. Add the tomatoes and cook for about 10 minutes. Add enough water to cover the lobster heads, toss in the thyme and oregano sprigs, raise heat to high, and bring to a boil. Reduce heat to low and simmer for an additional 45 minutes.

Strain out the lobster heads and discard, then return the broth to the pan. Pour in the chicken stock, raise heat to medium-low, and continue to cook until the stock is thick enough to coat the back of a spoon, about 20 minutes.

FOR SERVING:

Kosher salt

2 tablespoons sliced garlic

¼ teaspoon crushed red pepper

½ cup (120 ml) extra-virgin olive oil

6 (5-ounce/140 g) portions Fresh Pici (page 98)

1 recipe Lobster Stock (see opposite)

2½ cups (about 1.5 kg) lobster meat, chopped into bite-sized pieces

2 tablespoons chopped fresh tarragon

Bring a large pot of heavily salted water to boil. (The water should have the salinity of broth.)

While you wait for the water to boil, put the garlic, crushed red pepper, and half of the olive oil in a large sauté pan and sweat the garlic over medium heat for 5 minutes. When the water boils, add the pici and cook until just shy of al dente (about 75 percent done), 3 to 4 minutes. Drain the pasta. (Do not rinse it.)

Remove the lobster meat from the stock, then add the liquid stock and the cooked pasta to the pan and cook for about 1 minute, stirring to distribute the pasta so it soaks up the stock evenly. Add the lobster meat to the pan and cook for 1 minute more, while stirring. When the lobster is warmed through, add remaining ¼ cup (60 ml) olive oil and stir to combine. Remove from heat and stir in the tarragon. Serve immediately.

PACCHERI WITH PORK RAGÙ AND CACIOCAVALLO CHEESE

This dish is inspired by the ragùs my mother made when we were growing up, but it's a slightly stripped down version. Whereas her ragùs included ribs or lamb in addition to pork, this version uses only pork butt and pancetta, just because I happen to love the way those ingredients cook with tomato sauce. Paccheri is a tube-shaped pasta from southern Italy frequently used in Neapolitan cooking. It's similar in shape to a rigatoni, but with a smooth exterior that makes it a little more refined—a nice contrast to the homey, rustic character of the ragù.

Prep Note: The ragù requires a minimum of 2 hours of cooking time and yields double what you need for the pasta recipe below. It is not advised that you halve the recipe, but the unused portion can hold in the freezer in an airtight container for up to 1 month.

Serves 6

PORK RAGÙ:

Makes 1 quart (960 ml)

1 pound 5 ounces (595 g) boneless pork shoulder blade roast (fresh pork butt)

Kosher salt

3 ounces (85 g) pancetta

½ cup (65 g) minced onion

½ cup (30 g) minced carrot

¼ cup (25 g) minced celery

2 cloves garlic, minced

1 (15-ounce/430 g) can whole peeled tomatoes, preferably San Marzanos

Pinch crushed red pepper, plus more to taste

2 cups (480 ml) chicken stock, plus additional as needed

5 or 6 fresh basil leaves

TRIM AND DICE THE PORK BUTT, then sprinkle it with a little salt. Dice the pancetta.

In a large heavy braising pan or Dutch oven, sear the pieces of pork butt until they are nicely browned, about 10 minutes. Remove the pork butt and skim off the fat.

In the same pot set over low to medium heat, add the pancetta and cook until rendered, about 5 minutes. Add the onion, carrot, celery, and garlic and continue to cook until the vegetables are caramelized, about 10 minutes. While the vegetables are cooking, squeeze the tomatoes, then break them up a little bit with your hands. Add the tomatoes and their juice and cook until the pan is almost dry, about 12 minutes. Add the cubes of pork, the crushed red pepper, and stock and bring to a boil. (The pork should be submerged, so add additional stock if needed.) Stir in the basil leaves.

Cover and simmer over low heat for 1½ to 2 hours, until the pork is tender. Skim off excess grease, taste, adjust the flavor with salt and crushed red pepper, and prepare with the pasta according to the directions below. (The extra ragù will last for up to 1 week in the refrigerator, or can be frozen and stored for up to 1 month.)

Recipe continues

1 pound (455 g) dried paccheri or rigatoni

6 cloves garlic, thinly sliced

1 teaspoon crushed red pepper

¼ cup (60 ml) extra-virgin olive oil

1 teaspoon dried oregano

¼ cup (60 ml) dry white wine

2 cups (500 g) Pork Ragù (page 82)

1 cup (240 ml) Pomodoro Sauce (page 64)

6 tablespoons (85 g) unsalted butter

2 tablespoons chopped fresh flat-leaf parsley

6 tablespoons (40 g) grated Parmigiano-Reggiano cheese

¼ cup (25 g) grated caciocavallo cheese (use the large holes of a box grater)

Bring a pot of heavily salted water to a boil. (The water should have the salinity of broth.) Add the paccheri.

While the pasta is cooking, combine the garlic, crushed red pepper, and extra-virgin olive oil in a sauté pan set over medium heat. Cook until the garlic is lightly cooked but not dark in color. Add oregano and quickly deglaze the pan with the white wine, scraping up any bits that have stuck to the bottom of the pan. Add the pork ragù and pomodoro sauce. When the pasta is just shy of al dente (after about 75 percent of the cook time listed on the package), remove ½ cup (120 ml) of the pasta cooking water, then drain the paccheri. (Do not rinse.) Add the pasta and a few tablespoons of the cooking water to the sauté pan, stir to coat, adding additional cooking water to thin the sauce as needed.

Remove from heat then add the butter, parsley, and Parmigiano and stir to combine. Divide the pasta into individual serving bowls and finish each portion with about 3 teaspoons of the shaved caciocavallo. Serve immediately.

SCIALATIELLI WITH STEWED OCTOPUS

This is one of my favorite ways to eat octopus: braised in sauce, so that it releases a ton of flavor (and a beautiful purplish color) into the sauce as it cooks, which becomes deliciously concentrated as it reduces. (If you have any leftover after making the pasta, I highly recommend grabbing some crusty bread to sop it up, or making a little stewed octopus bruschetta for a snack.) Scialatielli is a pasta from Sorrento that is distinctive because of the inclusion of milk (and sometimes some basil and black pepper) in the dough; it is frequently paired with fish or seafood.

Serves 6

STEWED OCTOPUS SAUCE:

¼ cup (60 ml) extra-virgin olive oil

2 cups (110 g) thinly sliced onions (about 2 medium onions)

4 cloves garlic, very thinly sliced

1 teaspoon crushed red pepper

2 tablespoons capers, rinsed if salted

2 anchovy fillets, well rinsed and chopped

2 fresh plum or Roma tomatoes, seeded and chopped

2 pounds (910 g) cleaned octopus tentacles

Pinch kosher salt

⅓ cup (75 ml) dry white wine

2¼ cups (545 g) canned whole peeled tomatoes, with their juice

1 tablespoon chopped oregano

PREHEAT THE OVEN to 375°F (190°C).

In a large saucepan with a lid, heat the olive oil over medium-high heat, then add the onions, garlic, red pepper flakes, capers, and anchovies. Cook, stirring occasionally and adjusting the heat as necessary, until the onions are browned, about 7 minutes. Add the fresh tomatoes and stir to combine. Add the octopus tentacles and any residual liquid from the octopus. Season very lightly with salt (be aware this recipe contains a number of salty ingredients) and stir to combine.

Pour in the wine and cook, stirring occasionally, until the alcohol is cooked off, about 5 minutes.

Add the canned tomatoes, then press them with the back of a spoon to break them up. Add the oregano and bring the mixture to a boil. Continue to cook at a boil for another 5 minutes, then cover the pan and transfer it to the oven.

Cook, covered, for 30 minutes, then remove the cover and cook until the octopus is tender enough to be cut with the side of a spoon. (The time this takes will vary considerably depending on the thickness of the octopus tentacles; from as few as 10 minutes to up to 45 minutes.) Check the tentacles' tenderness every 10 minutes or so.

When the tentacles are done cooking, remove the pan from the oven. Remove the octopus from the sauce and set aside to cool. (Cooled octopus is easier to chop.) Meanwhile, pass the sauce through a food mill or fine-mesh sieve while still warm. Once the octopus has cooled to room temperature, chop it into pieces ¼ inch long (slice the heads more thinly), return it to the sauce, cover the pan, and refrigerate until ready to use. (The octopus and the sauce can be cooked up to 2 days ahead.)

Recipe continues

FOR SERVING:

Kosher salt

1 recipe Stewed Octopus Sauce (see above)

1 pound (455 g) dried scialatielli

3 tablespoons chopped pitted black olives

1 tablespoon plus 1 teaspoon chopped fresh oregano

½ cup (25 g) chopped fresh flat-leaf parsley

2 tablespoons chopped fresh basil

Bring a large pot of heavily salted water to a boil. (The water should have the salinity of broth.) Add the pasta.

While the scialatielli is cooking, heat the stewed octopus sauce in a large skillet set over medium heat.

When the pasta is just shy of al dente (after about 75 percent of the cooking time listed on the package), remove about ½ cup (120 ml) of the pasta-cooking liquid, then drain the pasta. (Do not rinse it.)

Add the pasta to the sauce followed by the olives, oregano, and parsley and stir to combine. (Add the reserved pasta cooking water a few tablespoons at a time to thin the sauce, as needed.)

When the sauce and octopus are combined, transfer to a serving platter, top with the basil, and serve immediately.

GNOCCHI WITH CLAMS

Spaghetti with clams is a classic and for a good reason: When done right, it's a dish that is rich with nostalgia for anyone who has enjoyed summer days by the sea. (It also has been part of my repertoire longer than almost any other dish, since I first learned to cook it at the Sea Loft, where I worked when I was sixteen.) Pairing the clams with gnocchi instead of spaghetti ups the ante because you can get that much more intensity of flavor in each bite by spearing a clam and a similarly sized dumpling together, as well as creating a really interesting texture and mouthfeel. And gnocchi, unlike other fresh pasta doughs, doesn't need to rest in the refrigerator overnight, so you can prepare and enjoy this dish immediately after you've finished making the dough.

Note: This recipe calls for manila clams, but you could easily substitute littlenecks or cockles.

Serves 6 to 8

½ cup (120 ml) extra-virgin olive oil, plus additional to taste

10 cloves garlic, 4 cloves smashed and 6 cloves thinly sliced

2 shallots, thinly sliced

1 sprig thyme

1½ teaspoons crushed red pepper

5 pounds (2.3 kg) manila clams, washed

1 cup (240 ml) dry white wine

6 green onions, light green and white parts only, thinly sliced

Kosher salt

1 recipe Gnocchi (page 95)

¼ cup (25 g) chopped fresh flat-leaf parsley

2 teaspoons Toasted Breadcrumbs (page 67)

HEAT ¼ CUP (60 ML) OF THE OLIVE OIL in a large sauté pan with a lid over medium-high heat. Add the smashed garlic and the shallots and sweat them for 8 minutes, stirring continuously to prevent them from browning.

Add the thyme and 1 teaspoon of the crushed red pepper, then the clams. Cook for 2 to 3 minutes then deglaze the pan with the white wine, scraping up any brown bits from the bottom. Cover the pan and steam until the clams open, 5 to 7 minutes. Strain through a fine-mesh sieve, reserving the cooking liquid (set aside ½ cup [120 ml] of the clam cooking liquid for later). Pick the clam meat from the shells, discarding any clams that have not opened, and reserve the meat in the remaining cooking liquid while you prepare the pasta.

Bring a pot of heavily salted water to a boil. (The water should have the salinity of broth.)

While you wait for the water to boil, put the sliced garlic, the remaining ½ teaspoon red pepper flakes, and the green onions in the same sauté pan you cooked the clams in. Add the remaining ¼ cup (60 ml) olive oil, and cook until the green onions have wilted and the garlic is lightly browned. Deglaze the pan with the reserved ½ cup (60 ml) clam cooking liquid.

When the water has boiled, add the gnocchi and cook for 3 minutes. Remove about ½ cup (60 ml) of the cooking water, then drain the gnocchi. (Do not rinse it.) Add the gnocchi and clams to the pan, along with about ¼ cup (60 ml) of the pasta cooking water, and cook for 3 to 4 minutes, stirring constantly, until the gnocchi and clams are warmed through. (Add some of the reserved pasta water to emulsify the oil and starch, if needed.) Remove from heat, stir in the parsley, and season with salt to taste. Top with the breadcrumbs, or serve with the breadcrumbs on the side.

BOLOGNESE WITH PARMIGIANO-REGGIANO FONDUTA

I learned how to make this Bolognese from a real Bolognese (a guy from Bologna) ages ago, and over the years, I've nailed down some tips and tricks that are integral to its success. First, when you are sautéing the beef with the mirepoix, really reduce it, so the juices completely evaporate and everything caramelizes in the beef fat; then add the wine and reduce again, until it's completely dry—that's what really concentrates the flavor. Second, do not grind the meat too finely—it should be coarser than hamburger meat. This gives it a nicer, much more palatable texture, not a grainy one. Third, this is the rare instance where you do not want to use an extra-virgin olive oil; there are a lot of subtleties in a Bolognese, so it requires a more neutral-flavored oil. The Parmigiano-Reggiano fonduta punctuates this decadent dish with another flavor profile, and is honestly just too good to leave out.

Serves 6

Prep Note: The Bolognese requires a minimum of 3 hours cooking time.

BOLOGNESE:

Makes about 1 quart (960 ml)

2 stalks celery

1 medium carrot

1 medium onion

2 ounces (55 g) pancetta, cut into chunks

6 ounces (170 g) veal stew meat, such as shoulder meat

6 ounces (170 g) beef stew meat, such as chuck

6 ounces (170 g) pork stew meat, such as shoulder or butt

¼ cup (60 ml) neutral-flavored olive oil (do not use extra-virgin)

Kosher salt and freshly ground black pepper

1 cup (240 ml) dry white wine

1 cup (240 ml) canned puréed tomatoes, preferably San Marzanos

1 quart (960 ml) chicken stock

IF YOU HAVE A MEAT GRINDER, using a medium grinding disc, grind the celery, carrot, onion, and pancetta. (I like a medium grind, which means the holes are about the size of my pinky fingernail.) Set aside, then grind the veal, beef, and pork (or have the butcher do it for you).

If you don't have a grinder, chop the celery, onion, carrot, and pancetta by hand into a small dice and set aside. Add the veal, beef, and pork to a food processor, and using a blade (not a disc), pulse the meat until it just begins to break apart, erring on the side of larger rather than smaller pieces. (Alternatively, chop the vegetables yourself, but have a butcher coarsely grind the meat.)

Heat the oil in a Dutch oven or a deep heavy-bottomed pot over medium heat. Add the celery, carrot, onion, and pancetta to the pot and sauté until the vegetables are lightly browned, about 15 minutes. Season the ground meat with salt and pepper, add it to the pot, and increase the heat to high; cook until everything is nicely browned. (The meat will release a lot of liquid initially, which will evaporate, and then everything will cook in the meat's fat.) Pour in the wine and cook until the wine evaporates almost completely and the pan looks dry, about 10 minutes. Add the tomatoes and cook until the mixture darkens considerably and begins to look dry, about 12 minutes.

Add the chicken stock and cook, uncovered, over very low heat until the meat is very tender and full of flavor, about 3 hours. Prepare with the pasta as described below, or cover and refrigerate until ready to use. (The Bolognese will last for up to 3 days in the refrigerator, or in an airtight container in the freezer for up to 1 month.)

Recipe continues

Parmigiano-Reggiano Fonduta

Makes 1½ cups (360 ml)

Note: This recipe yields double what you will need for the pasta dish below, but the leftover can be served on the side, or saved as a dip for crusty bread.

1 cup (240 ml) heavy cream

1¼ cups (125 g) grated Parmigiano-Reggiano cheese

1 tablespoon extra-virgin olive oil

Pour the cream in a small pot and bring to a boil.

When the cream has reduced by half, transfer to a blender with the cheese and olive oil and blend until smooth. Serve warm.

FOR SERVING:

1 recipe fresh Tagliatelle (page 99)

1 recipe Bolognese sauce (page 90)

¼ teaspoon crushed red pepper

2½ cups Pomodoro Sauce (page 64)

3 tablespoons unsalted butter

1½ cups (150 g) grated Parmigiano-Reggiano cheese

2 tablespoons extra-virgin olive oil

Kosher salt

¾ cup (240 ml) Parmigiano-Reggiano Fonduta (left)

Bring a pot of heavily salted water to a boil. (The water should have the salinity of broth.)

While you wait for the water to boil, add the Bolognese, red pepper flakes, and pomodoro sauce to a sauté pan and cook on medium-low heat, stirring to combine, until the sauce is reduced by about one-fourth and the pan looks quite dry. When the water boils, add the pasta and cook until just shy of al dente (about 75 percent done), about 3 minutes. Remove about ½ cup (120 ml) of the pasta cooking water, then drain the pasta. (Do not rinse it.) Add the drained tagliatelle and a few tablespoons of the cooking water to the Bolognese and toss to coat, adding additional cooking water as needed so the fat and starch emulsifies.

Remove from heat, then add the butter, Parmigiano-Reggiano, and olive oil. Season to taste with salt, then serve immediately with drizzles of fonduta on top.

PASTA AND GNOCCHI DOUGH

Making fresh pasta dough takes a little bit of getting used to, but it's such a rewarding skill for a home cook to have in their repertoire. Here are a couple of tips to set you up for success:

- Make your dough well in advance, at least a day ahead of when you plan to use it. (With the exception of the gnocchi and gnudi, which you can cook right away.) Letting your dough rest before you shape it will make it easier to work with; I also freeze shaped pasta such as the cavatelli after the shapes have been cut, because if you cook it when it's too fresh, the pieces swell up.

- If possible, try to weigh the flour in grams, rather than measuring it in cups. It's more accurate.

- Be specific about flour selection. Different flours have different protein compositions and gluten strengths, which affects the texture of the finished pasta. Double zero (00) flour and semolina are the most common flours used in pasta making. (In Italy, the number refers to the coarseness of the grind, with 00 being the most finely ground, and 2 being the coarsest.) These flours are readily available online, in specialty markets, and even at some supermarket chains. Seek them out, and avoid substituting all-purpose flour if possible.

- Test cook your dough before you shape it all, especially for dumplings like the gnocchi and gnudi, to make sure the pasta doesn't fall apart in the water. Years ago, William Grimes, who was the restaurant critic for the *New York Times* then, walked into a restaurant I was working in and ordered gnocchi. Turns out the guy at the pasta station hadn't tested it, so you can imagine my horror when the gnocchi fell apart in the cooking water. We had to cook each piece with a slotted spoon very, very carefully to make sure the critic got presentable-looking gnocchi. Learn from my mistakes.

CAVATELLI

Makes six 5-ounce (140 g) portions

12 ounces (340 g) ricotta cheese, plus additional to keep the dough moist, as needed

225 grams double zero (00) flour (about 1¾ cups, though see note on page 93), plus more for shaping the pasta

80 grams semolina flour (about ½ cup, though see note on page 93)

¾ teaspoon kosher salt

Place all the ingredients into the bowl of a stand mixer fitted with a paddle attachment and mix until just combined. (If the dough looks crumbly and dry, add a little more ricotta.) Take the dough out of the bowl and wrap tightly in plastic wrap. Let the dough rest at room temperature for a minimum of 8 hours, or refrigerate overnight.

When ready to make the pasta, remove the plastic wrap and cut the dough into 6 equal slices. Cover 5 of the slices with plastic wrap, then, using your hands, roll out the sixth slice into a long, ½-inch-thick (12 mm) rope of dough. Cut the rope into pieces that are 1 to 1½ inches (2.5 to 4 cm) long.

You can shape the dough using either a gnocchi board or a knife.

To shape with a gnocchi board: Lightly dust the gnocchi board with 00 flour, then place a piece of dough in the middle of the board. Carefully push into the surface of the dough using your thumb, and while pushing into the dough, roll down so that the pasta curls around itself. (If you use too much force, the pasta will tear, and if you use too little force, the pasta won't curl on to itself.) The final shape should resemble a caterpillar: small, cylindrical, with ridges in the sides. Repeat with the rest of the dough pieces.

To shape with a knife: Place the tip of a small kitchen knife on top of one of the pieces of cut dough; the blade should be flat across the top, with the cutting edge facing away from you. Press the knife into the dough as you pull the dough toward you; the dough will curl in around itself. Carefully remove the dough from the blade, using your thumb to very gently push it down from the edge, without disrupting the fold. (The final shape should resemble a caterpillar, small and cylindrical, though it will not have ridges.) Repeat with the rest of the dough pieces.

Place the shaped cavatelli on a lightly floured cookie sheet, then repeat with the remaining slices of dough.

GNOCCHI

Makes 6 portions

1¾ pounds (800 g) Idaho potatoes, peels on

Kosher salt

2 egg yolks, from large eggs

1⅓ cups (155 g) double zero (00) flour, plus extra to work the dough

Preheat the oven to 350°F (175°C)

Prick the potatoes a few times around the surface area with a fork and bake for about 1 hour, until cooked through.

Cut the potatoes in half crosswise and push them through a tamis or ricer into a mixing bowl. (Do not use a food mill—it will break up the starches and make the potatoes very gummy.) Season with salt and set aside.

In a small bowl, mix the egg yolks with a little bit of salt. Sift the flour over the potatoes and mix in the flour gently with your hands by lifting the riced potatoes then letting the pieces fall through your fingers. Drizzle the egg yolk mixture over the top and mix it into dough, then knead briefly until evenly combined.

Roll the dough into logs that are a manageable length to work with. Pick out one piece of dough and cover the rest with a kitchen towel. Roll the first piece out to approximately ½ inch (12 mm) in diameter, then cut the dough into individual pieces about 1 inch (2.5 cm) long.

To shape, place one piece of cut gnocchi dough on a clean counter and, using a fork, roll the dough down the back side of the fork, starting from the top of the tines, to create a rolled, ridged shape. (You can also shape with a gnocchi board, using the same technique.) Place the finished gnocchi on a floured cookie sheet as you go. Repeat until all the dough has been cut and shaped.

The gnocchi can be cooked immediately, or placed on a cookie sheet and frozen until firm, then transferred to a ziptight bag and returned to the freezer.

GNUDI

Makes 6 portions (about 40 gnudi)

2 cups (490 g) sheep's milk ricotta

2 egg yolks from large eggs

¼ cup (50 g) finely chopped blanched spinach

½ cup (50 g) grated Parmigiano-Reggiano cheese

¼ cup (30 g) all-purpose flour

3 tablespoons panko

1 teaspoon freshly grated nutmeg

Kosher salt and freshly ground black pepper

Semolina flour, for dusting and coating the gnudi

Combine the ricotta, egg yolks, spinach, Parmigiano, all-purpose flour, panko, and nutmeg. Let the dough rest for 10 minutes.

Using a cookie scoop, roll the dough into balls a little smaller than golf balls. Coat a baking sheet liberally with semolina flour, place the gnudi on top of the semolina, then sprinkle more semolina on top. Refrigerate, uncovered, for 12 hours or overnight before using.

MACCHERONI OR SPAGHETTI DOUGH

Makes about six 5-ounce (140 g) portions

9 egg yolks from large eggs

1 large egg

2 tablespoons extra-virgin olive oil

½ teaspoon kosher salt

3¼ cups (405 g) double zero (00) flour

⅓ cup (45 g) semolina flour

Special equipment: pasta roller

Put the egg yolks, egg, olive oil, salt, and ⅓ cup (75 ml) water in a bowl and mix with a whisk. In a separate bowl, whisk together the 00 flour and the semolina.

Pour the egg yolk mixture into the bowl of a stand mixer fitted with a dough hook. Add the flour mixture one-third at a time and mix on medium-low speed, adding the next third once the previous third has been incorporated, 6 to 8 minutes total. The dough should be very smooth, but not sticky looking; if it looks dry or crumbly, add a little bit of water to moisten it and bring it together. Remove the dough from the mixer bowl, wrap tightly in plastic wrap, and let rest for at least 1 hour, or ideally overnight.

When ready to cut the pasta, unwrap the dough and slice it into 8 pieces. Cover 7 of the pieces with a kitchen towel. Take the remaining piece and roll it through the pasta roller on the #7 setting. Fold the sheet into thirds by bringing one end into the center and the other end over it.

Feed the folded dough into the machine, with the folded edges to the side. Repeat the folding into thirds, then feed the dough through the pasta roller with the folded edges towards the rollers. Set the sheet of pasta aside, cover it, and repeat with the rest of the pieces of dough.

Pair off the sheets by placing one on top of another (you will now have 4 sheets in all). Roll each double sheet through the roller. Repeat the pairing off of sheets (so now you have two sheets), and feed each of these sheets through the roller. Repeat one more time so you end up with one long sheet of pasta, flouring the dough as needed as you go.

Set the roller to #5. Cut the dough in half, place one half on top of the other, then cut in half again, so you end up with 2 sheets of pasta that are roughly hand length. Cut each of these stacks in half horizontally so you have 4 sheets in all.

For Spaghetti: Pass each sheet through an Imperia 2-millimeter cutter or a spaghetti-cutting attachment on a stand mixer. Freeze for at least an hour before cooking. (The pasta will last in the freezer for up to a month.)

For Maccheroni: Take each sheet and, using a rolling pin or pasta roller, roll it out to about 4 inches (10 cm) long and ¼ inch thick, then cut the dough into strands about ¼ inch wide. Freeze for at least 1 hour before cooking. (The pasta will last in the freezer for up to a month.)

PICI

Makes six 6-ounce (170 g) portions

3½ cups (405 g) double zero (00) flour

2½ cups durum flour

2 tablespoons kosher salt

2 tablespoons extra-virgin olive oil

Mix the 00 flour, semolina, and salt together in the bowl of a stand mixer fitted with a dough hook attachment. Bring 2 cups (480 ml) water to a boil and gradually pour it into the flour mixture, mixing as you go until it is smooth and supple. Wrap the dough in plastic wrap while it's warm and refrigerate for 24 hours.

When ready to cook, divide the dough into 4 equal pieces. Cover 3 with plastic wrap to prevent them from drying out while you work with the first.

Using a rolling pin or a dowel, roll out the uncovered piece of dough until it is ¼ inch thick.

Using a knife, a pastry wheel, or a pizza cutter roll, cut the dough into strands 5 to 8 inches (12 to 20 cm) long and ¼ inch wide. (Have a clean, damp cloth at the ready, which you can use to wipe down your work surface if the dough gets dry and is difficult to roll out.) On a lightly floured work surface, take each strand of pasta, and press in the edges with your pinkies to taper the ends. Repeat with the remaining pieces of dough.

TAGLIATELLE

Note: This dough can also be used to make the Tajarin on page 168 or the Raviolini on page 169.

Makes six 5-ounce (140 g) portions

1 kilogram double zero (00) flour (about 8 cups, but see note on page 93), plus more as needed for shaping and cutting the dough

1 tablespoon kosher salt

3 tablespoons extra-virgin olive oil

13 large eggs, whisked together

Special equipment: pasta roller

Place the flour and salt in the bowl of a stand mixer fitted with a dough hook. Begin to mix at lowest speed as you add the olive oil. Gradually add the eggs and mix until a dough is formed, adding a little water to moisten the dough if it's dry.

Remove the dough from mixing bowl and knead for 7 minutes, adding more flour if the dough is too sticky. The dough should be smooth and supple, not wet. Once the dough is smooth, wrap it tightly with plastic wrap and let it rest for at least 1 hour.

Unwrap the dough and cut it into 6 pieces. Cover 5 of the pieces with plastic wrap so they do not dry out. Flatten out the uncovered piece of dough, and then, using either a pasta roller or pasta roller attachment for a stand mixer, feed it through the roller at the thickest setting.

Once the pasta has gone through the roller, fold the dough in half and push it through again. Fold it in half one more time and push it through a final time. When the dough is rolled out to the width of the roller, fold the dough in thirds (by folding in one edge of the dough to the centerline then placing the other edge on top). Turn the dough and push through the roller again. (You are trying to get a uniform square or rectangular shape.) Repeat this process until the dough is just shy of the width of the pasta roller.

Turn the dial on the pasta roller to #2 and roll the dough through one time, then turn to #3 and roll the dough through one time.

Once the sheet of pasta is rolled out, place it on a clean counter dusted lightly with 00 flour. Lightly dust some flour onto the dough, then roll both of the ends of the pasta sheet towards the middle until they meet. Using a sharp chef's knife, cut strips of pasta to your desired thickness (¼ to ½ inch [12 mm] thick). Once the pasta is cut, place a dowel under the dough (in the middle where the two ends met when you rolled the pasta), pull the dough up, and the cut pasta will just unravel. (Alternately, if you have a fettuccine cutter or attachment, you can use that to cut the pasta after it has been passed through the roller the final time.) Dust with a little semolina flour and cook immediately.

CHAPTER 5

Fish *and* Seafood

Pasta may be what I'm best known for, but fish is also close to my heart. As mentioned previously, my first cooking job was at a restaurant in my hometown called the Sea Loft, where I made vats of chowder, fried endless clam strips, and fell in love with kitchen life. Later, when I finally made it to Italy and visited the beach kiosks in seaside towns along the Adriatic coast, one of my greatest revelations there was how simply you could treat a fish and still produce stunning results.

Fish is intimidating for some home cooks, but it really shouldn't be. It's satisfying, healthy, and doesn't need fancy ingredients, a lot of time, or complicated cooking techniques as long as you are working with high-quality protein. Which is not to say that some of the more elaborate preparations in this chapter, inspired by my Sea Loft days, aren't a blast to pull off. (When we were testing the recipes for this book, I texted a picture of the Stuffed Lobster [page 116] to my friend Mo Collins, who worked at the Sea Loft with me. He wrote back saying that he still makes them all the time and people go crazy for them!)

BRANZINO ALL'ACQUA PAZZA

Acqua pazza means "crazy water," and this dish was crazy popular when I worked at San Domenico. It's a delicious, brothy flavor bomb, combining spice, heat, and herbal notes with the taste of the sea. My version includes lobster meat along with the branzino, in addition to the shells that are traditionally used in the preparation of the broth. I'm a big fan of layering proteins to give more complexity to a dish, rather than adding a lot of different spices and ingredients. The addition of lobster adds a level of richness without interfering with the strong, fresh flavors of the branzino and *acqua pazza*. You could pair this with any grains that will soak up that crazy, savory broth, but I like to use couscous—the quinoa of the nineties—just as we did in the restaurant.

Serves 4

2 tablespoons extra-virgin olive oil, plus additional as needed

2 cloves garlic, sliced ¼ inch thick

Kosher salt

Pinch crushed red pepper

½ cup thinly sliced zucchini, cut into moons ⅛ inch thick

½ cup (75 g) cherry tomatoes, quartered

1 recipe Acqua Pazza Broth (see below)

½ cup (290 g) lobster meat, blanched, removed from shell, and chopped into ½-inch (12 mm) pieces

4 branzino fillets (6 to 7 ounces [170 to 200 g] each), with skin

Freshly ground black pepper

¼ cup (10 g) chopped fresh basil, plus additional for garnish

3 tablespoons chopped fresh flat-leaf parsley, plus additional for garnish

1 cup (190 g) couscous, cooked according to package directions

HEAT 1 TABLESPOON OF THE OLIVE OIL in a large sauté pan over medium-high heat. Add the garlic, salt to taste, a pinch of red pepper flakes, the zucchini, and cherry tomatoes and cook until the pectin from the tomatoes releases, about 3 minutes. Using a fine-mesh sieve, strain the acqua pazza broth over the tomatoes. Add the blanched lobster meat, and when the lobster is heated through (about a minute or two), add basil, parsley, and salt to taste. Add a little olive oil, then reduce the heat to low while you cook the branzino.

Pat the fillets dry and season the branzino with salt and black pepper. In a sauté pan over medium-high heat, add the remaining tablespoon olive oil, and sear the branzino, skin side down, until the skin is crispy, about 4 minutes. Turn the fish and cook for an additional minute.

Divide the couscous among four wide shallow bowls. Place one branzino fillet, skin side up, on top of each mound of couscous. Ladle the finished sauce with the tomatoes, zucchini, and lobster over the top. Garnish with parsley and basil and serve immediately.

Recipe continues

Acqua Pazza Broth

1 tablespoon extra-virgin olive oil

1½ onions, sliced into half-moons

1 head garlic, cloves peeled and thinly sliced

8 plum or Roma tomatoes, chopped

Pinch crushed red pepper

Kosher salt

2 cups canned San Marzano whole peeled tomatoes, hand-crushed

2 cups (240 ml) dry white wine

4 branzino bodies, gills removed, soaked in ice water

4 lobster bodies (knuckles, claws, and tail)

1 cup (40 g) loosely packed fresh basil leaves

In a wide shallow pan (such as a rondeau), heat 1 tablespoon of the olive oil over medium heat.

Add the onions and sweat for 6 minutes, then add the garlic and cook until fragrant and toasted, about 2 minutes. Add the chopped fresh tomatoes, red pepper flakes, and salt to taste, then cook on medium heat until the tomatoes release their liquid, about 5 minutes.

Add the San Marzano tomatoes, lower the heat to medium-low, and cook until the mixture is reduced by half, about 30 minutes. Add the white wine, keeping the heat at medium-low, and reduce by half again, about 30 minutes.

Add the bones from the branzino bodies to the tomato mixture. Cover the surface of the pan with ice, skim out any impurities that rise up, bring to a boil, then reduce the heat and simmer for 20 minutes.

Add the lobster bodies and continue cooking on low for another 20 minutes. Strain the broth through a cheesecloth or fine-mesh strainer. Return the broth to the stove and cook, uncovered, until it is reduced by one-third. Add the basil and simmer for an additional 10 minutes. Set aside until you're ready to serve.

ROASTED FRESH OYSTERS WITH NDUJA

When we were doing the recipe testing for the book, I couldn't stop eating these oysters—I finally had to push them on my neighbor for fear that I would devour them all myself. In my opinion, ingredients that make you work for them, like these oysters, which must be shucked, had better be worth what you end up with, and this preparation passed that test with flying colors. Traditionally, nduja, a very spicy, peppery, spreadable sausage, isn't cooked at all, but I love the way that it melts into the oysters in the oven. That smooth, spicy flavor punctuated by the slight crunch of the panko breadcrumbs is all that you need to make that shucking feel worthwhile.

Serves 4 to 6 as an appetizer

12 fresh oysters

12 ounces (340 g) nduja, casing removed (if you can't find nduja, you can substitute fresh chorizo)

2 tablespoons chopped fresh flat-leaf parsley

4 tablespoons (20 g) panko

¼ cup (½ stick/55 g) cold unsalted butter, cut into 12 cubes

1 lemon, sliced into wedges

PREHEAT THE OVEN to 375°F (190°C).

Shuck the oysters on the half shell, then place them on a baking sheet and chill in the refrigerator while you prepare the nduja.

In a bowl, combine the nduja and chopped parsley. Place 2 tablepoons of the sausage mixture on top of each oyster. Sprinkle 1 teaspoon panko on top of each oyster, then place 1 teaspoon butter on top of the breadcrumbs. Bake for 15 minutes, until the tops are golden brown.

Remove from oven and place the oysters on a large platter. Add the lemon wedges in between the oysters and serve immediately.

FISH TARTARE

This tartare is a simple combination of flavors that will showcase whatever fish it's paired with; as long as your fish is beautiful, you can take your pick: tuna, yellowtail, branzino, or sea bream all work well. You can use a whole fillet if you like, but at the restaurants (and now at home), I like to whip this up with whatever fish trimmings I have left over after preparing a larger dish. There are few things more satisfying for a chef—or home cook—than taking scraps and elevating them into something beautiful. (If you are feeling fancy, top this with a little caviar.)

Serves 4

10 ounces (280 g) fish trimmings (or fillet), finely diced

1 avocado, cut into small dice

1½ teaspoons chopped fresh flat-leaf parsley

½ teaspoon chile oil

1½ tablespoons extra-virgin olive oil

Kosher salt

20 slices breakfast radish (from 3 or 4 radishes)

Watercress leaves, for garnish

COMBINE THE FISH, avocado, parsley, and both oils in a bowl, mix well, then season with salt.

Divide the tartare among 4 plates, then add the radish slices on top. Garnish each plate with a few leaves of watercress and serve immediately.

HAMACHI CRUDO WITH GINGER OIL AND FINGER LIMES

When I started putting crudos on my menus in the late nineties, my customers had no idea what was going on—people started asking for chopsticks in an Italian restaurant! But they caught on because crudo, the Italian preparation of raw fish, is a delicious and healthy starter that really resonated with New York City diners once they tried it. I personally do not care for cooked hamachi—I think searing it gives it a bit of a metallic taste—but I love it raw and paired, as in this crudo, with a little bit of heat, a little bit of spice, and the pop of acidity from the limes.

Prep Note: This recipe calls for finger limes, which are known for the seeds contained in their tiny juice sacs, but you can substitute regular limes and supreme them to remove the skin and pith.

Serves 4 as an appetizer

8 ounces (225 g) sushi-grade hamachi (or another variety of yellowtail), thinly cut against the grain into 16 slices about ⅛ inch thick

1 recipe Ginger-Lime Oil (recipe follows)

Maldon salt or another flaky sea salt

16 Pickled Fresno Chiles (page 14), finely chopped

ARRANGE THE HAMACHI SLICES on a serving plate. Spoon about three-fourths of the ginger-lime oil over the fish (or enough to cover the top). Lightly sprinkle Maldon crystals over the fish, then spoon about ½ teaspoon of the chopped Fresno chiles on each slice. Serve immediately.

Ginger-Lime Oil

¼ cup (60 ml) extra-virgin olive oil

2 tablespoons thinly sliced fresh ginger

4 tablespoons (60 g) finger limes or supremed limes (see Prep Note, above)

In a small pot, heat the olive oil over low heat and stir in the sliced ginger. Remove from heat, cover with plastic wrap, and let sit for 12 hours or overnight at room temperature.

The next day, clean the finger limes (if using) and set aside.

The next morning, strain the oil through a fine-mesh sieve or cheesecloth, discarding the ginger, then add the finger limes (or the supremed limes) and mix. Use immediately, or cover and keep at room temperature until ready to use.

TUNA CRUDO WITH LEMON AND PICKLED FRESNOS

If you have some great tuna and you want to do as little to it as possible, this is the way to go—this recipe is all about letting the beautiful flavor of the fish shine. If I'm in the mood for a salad, sometimes I tweak the proportions of the recipe, adding more lettuce, then adding some of the liquid from the pickled Fresnos to the oil and lemon juice for the dressing.

Serves 4 as an appetizer

4 tablespoons (60 ml) extra-virgin olive oil

4 tablespoons (60 ml) lemon juice (from about 2 lemons)

Maldon salt or another flaky sea salt

8 to 10 ounces (225 to 280 g) raw sushi-grade tuna, sliced to yield about 20 pieces

20 leaves baby lettuce

20 slices Pickled Fresno Chiles (page 14), sliced into thin rings with seeds removed

20 slices breakfast radishes (from 3 to 4 radishes)

IN A MIXING BOWL, combine the extra-virgin olive oil, lemon juice, and some flaky sea salt to taste. Drizzle the vinaigrette over the tuna.

Place the baby lettuce on a serving plate (or divide among four individual plates). Arrange the marinated tuna around the lettuce, and place the chile slices on top of the tuna. Add the radish slices, and drizzle the remaining marinade over the top. Add salt flakes to taste and serve immediately.

CLAM CHOWDER

We ate a lot of chowder growing up—always, of course, the white New England variety. Traditionally, New England clam chowder has a ton of cream in it, but I wanted to develop a lighter version that didn't rely so heavily on dairy. Instead, I purée some of the potatoes, because the soft purée adds its own creaminess that can replace some of the milk. (I also use chunks of purple potato, because I think their bright color makes the dish look fresher, though if you can't find purple potatoes, you can use the same quantity of regular potatoes.) For the purists out there, this recipe still includes the option of adding some cream, but I prefer the cleaner flavor of this soup when dairy is omitted entirely, and just finish the chowder with a little extra-virgin olive oil.

Serves 8 to 10 (about 2 quarts/1.9 liters)

¼ cup diced applewood-smoked bacon

1 tablespoon celery seed

3 cups (375 g) finely diced white or yellow onions (from about 2 medium onions)

1½ cups (150 g) finely diced celery

2 teaspoons kosher salt, plus additional to taste

Pinch crushed red pepper

¼ cup (60 ml) extra-virgin olive oil, plus more to finish, if desired

5 fresh live manila or littleneck clams, soaked in water with a little vinegar to remove sand

3 pounds (1.4 kg) red potatoes, peeled, two-thirds roughly chopped and one-third cut into ¼-inch dice

1 pound (455 g) peeled Peruvian potatoes (or other purple potatoes), cut into ¼-inch dice

1 quart (960 ml) canned clam juice or fish stock

1 cup (240 ml) scalded cream (optional)

¼ cup (17 g) chopped fresh flat-leaf parsley

ADD THE BACON to a large heavy-bottomed pot set on medium-low heat and render the fat for 10 to 12 minutes, making sure that the bacon does not burn or take on too much color. Add the celery seed, onions, celery, salt, and red pepper flakes to the bacon and sweat the vegetables for 5 to 8 minutes, until the onions are translucent but have not yet taken on any color.

While you are sweating the onions, in another large heavy-bottomed pot add the olive oil and the clams, cover, and cook on high heat until the clams start to open up, about 7 minutes. Once the clams are open (discard any that haven't), remove the pot from the heat. Using tongs, remove the clams from the cooking water. Reserve the cooking liquid, allow it to settle for a few minutes, then decant it to remove the sand.

When the clams are cool enough to handle, pick out the clam meat from the shells and discard the shells. Roughly chop the clam meat and reserve.

Add the roughly chopped red potatoes to the pot with the clam liquid and cook them on medium heat until the potatoes are tender, 8 to 10 minutes. Allow to cool slightly, then carefully transfer the potatoes and some of the cooking water to a blender and purée until completely smooth, adding more liquid as needed to achieve a consistency that is neither gummy nor watery. (Do not fill the blender more than two-thirds of the way to the top, as the steam from the hot liquid can cause the top to pop off.) Alternatively, you can use an immersion blender and purée in the pot.

Add the diced red and purple potatoes to the bacon and vegetables, then pour in the canned clam juice. Add the puréed potatoes, along with the chopped clams and the cup of cream (if using), and heat on medium-high until warmed through. Salt to taste. Add chopped parsley just before serving, and finish with extra-virgin olive oil, if desired.

GRILLED SWORDFISH WITH TOMATOES AND WATERCRESS

I adore a simple grilled fish: I love how this noninvasive cooking technique enhances the clean flavor of the ingredients that it is applied on, which, when you have great fish, is all you need. This combination of grilled fish with a bracing salsa-like accompaniment is a real winner for groups, dinner parties, backyard gatherings—anytime you want to please a crowd without spending hours in the kitchen. The swordfish could easily be swapped out for a different fish such as tuna, yellowtail, halibut, or even a freshwater fish. (I recently made this with a rainbow trout that I caught in Montana.) If you prefer seafood, grilled shrimp or lobster could sub in as well. You really can use whatever you want—the olive-tomato-oregano salsa complements pretty much anything that comes from the sea.

Serves 4 as a main course

3 plum tomatoes

2 to 3 tablespoons extra-virgin olive oil

1 cup (145 g) cherry tomatoes, cut in half

Kosher salt

12 black olives (such as Gaeta), pit removed, finely chopped

2 tablespoons drained capers (not salt-packed)

1½ teaspoons finely chopped fresh oregano

1½ teaspoons finely chopped basil

1½ teaspoons red wine vinegar

1 small bunch watercress, stems discarded

4 swordfish steaks, ¾ to 1 inch (2 to 2.5 cm) thick (6 to 8 ounces/170 to 225 g)

Flaky salt, such as Maldon, to finish

Special equipment: An instant-read thermometer

SLICE THE PLUM TOMATOES in half lengthwise. Gently squeeze the tomatoes into a fine-mesh strainer set over a small bowl. Reserve the juices and discard the seeds. Dice the tomatoes.

In a medium sauté pan, heat 1½ tablespoons olive oil over medium-high heat. Add the diced tomatoes, the cherry tomatoes, and the collected tomato juice to the pan. Season with a couple pinches of salt and cook, stirring occasionally to help the cherry tomatoes release their juices, 2 to 3 minutes. Add the olives, capers, oregano, basil, and vinegar and cook the salsa for an additional minute, stirring to combine all the ingredients, then remove from heat.

Wilt the watercress by heating a small sauté pan on medium heat with ½ tablespoon olive oil. Add the watercress and a pinch of salt and cook just until the greens are wilted.

For the swordfish, heat a grill (or a grill pan) to medium-high heat. Brush the swordfish with olive oil and season well with salt and pepper on both sides. Cook the fish 3 to 4 minutes on each side, until the internal temp reaches 130°F (55°C) (there should not be any color on the interior). While the fish cooks, reheat the watercress and the tomato mixture, if necessary.

Divide the tomato and olive salsa among four plates, top each with a piece of swordfish, then place the watercress on top of the fish. Lightly sprinkle flaky salt over the watercress and serve immediately.

STUFFED LOBSTER

My wife, Mel, adores stuffed lobster, so this recipe is dedicated to her. My associations with stuffed lobster hark back to the Sea Loft, my first restaurant job, where we made it with Ritz crackers and tons and tons of clarified butter. That's a bit rich for my taste these days (and for most people's), so in this version, I've replaced some of the butter with shrimp, crab meat, and stock, which add depth, and added panko breadcrumbs to the Ritz crackers. The result is a stuffed lobster that holds on to that taste of nostalgia, but with even more flavor (and less fat).

Prep Note: To make the Ritz cracker crumbs: Unwrap a sleeve of Ritz crackers and place them in a ziptight bag. Beat with a mortar or rolling pin until the crackers are broken down into small chunks about the size of a dime.

Serves 4

4 (1-pound/455 g) live Maine lobsters

1 cup plus 1 teaspoon kosher salt

1½ cups (190 g) finely diced onions

1 cup (2 sticks/225 g) unsalted butter

¼ cup (60 ml) extra-virgin olive oil, plus additional for brushing the lobster before serving

½ cup (50 g) finely diced celery

½ teaspoon crushed red pepper

1 tablespoon ground fennel seeds

1 tablespoon smoked paprika

15 peeled baby shrimp, cut into 1-inch (2.5 cm) pieces

⅜ cup (55 g) lump crab meat

2 cups (480 ml) Lobster Stock (page 81), thinned with a little water

2⅓ cups (170 g) Ritz cracker crumbs (see Prep Note above)

2 cups (160 g) panko

¼ cup (17 g) roughly chopped fresh flat-leaf parsley

¼ cup (10 g) chopped fresh basil

2 lemons

PREHEAT THE OVEN to 425°F (220°C).

In a large pot, bring 1½ gallons (5.7 liters) water and 1 cup of the salt to a boil. Add the lobsters, and when the water returns to a boil, cook the lobsters with the lid on for 1 minute (just enough time to kill them; you don't want the meat very cooked), then immediately take them out of the water and let cool to room temperature. (Do not shock with cold water, as that dulls the flavor.)

Once the lobsters are cool, cut them lengthwise down the middle but not all the way through, so each lobster will still be in one piece. Discard the vein and the cartilage, but reserve the greenish tomalley (lobster innards) for the stuffing.

Heat the butter and olive oil in a 2-quart/liter saucepan set over low heat. When the butter is melted, add the onions, celery, salt, crushed red pepper, fennel seed, and smoked paprika. Turn up the heat to medium-low and sweat the vegetables for about 10 minutes, then turn the heat down to low and continue to cook for 5 more minutes.

Add the shrimp, lump crab meat, and the seafood stock to the vegetables, along with the Ritz cracker crumbs, panko, basil, parsley, and the reserved tomalley, and mix until all ingredients are incorporated.

Place the lobsters on a baking sheet and evenly divide the stuffing to stuff the 4 lobsters, pressing the stuffing into the lobsters with the pressure you would use to crease a pie dough. (You want the stuffing to cook through, but you don't want the lobsters to overcook.) Brush the lobster shells with olive oil and squeeze the juice of ½ lemon on top of each lobster.

Bake the lobsters for 12 minutes, then raise the temperature and broil them for 3 minutes, or until the stuffing has developed a golden-brown crust. Serve immediately.

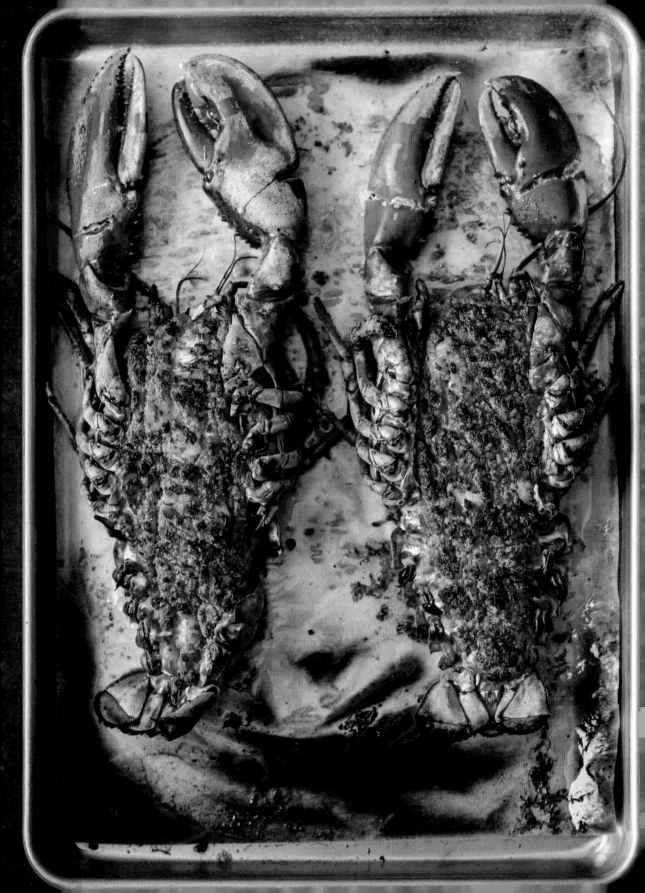

LOBSTER ROLL, BOTH WAYS

Obviously, there is a huge debate about which type of lobster roll is better: Connecticut or New England–style. Being from Connecticut, I am biased, of course: warm lobster over cold. For me, the CT-style wins because of how the lobster meat absorbs the butter sauce when it is poached. (You want the meat a bit under-cooked—just coming out of the shell—when you poach it, so the lobster finishes cooking as it warms in the butter sauce; that's what helps it retain its succulent flavor.) And don't skimp on the crunch on top. (As in the Stuffed Lobster recipe on page 116, I've combined crushed Ritz crackers with panko for the topping because I like the contrast between the two textures.) All of that said, my father was from Maine and the New England version was a staple of my child-hood summers, so even though I prefer the Connecticut preparation, I truly do love them both. In an ideal world, I would make a plate of one of each, so I could go back and forth. I encourage you to do the same.

Connecticut-Style Lobster Rolls

Serves 4

½ cup kosher salt, plus more for the butter sauce

2 (1¼- to 1½-pound/570 to 680 g) live Maine lobsters

1 cup (2 sticks/350 g) unsalted butter, cut into 1-inch (2.5 cm) cubes, plus additional for toasting the rolls

1 tablespoon cornstarch

⅓ cup (25 g) Ritz cracker crumbs (see Prep Note, page 116)

⅓ cup (25 g) panko

2 pinches cayenne pepper

¼ teaspoon paprika

Pinch granulated garlic

2 tablespoons extra-virgin olive oil

1 tablespoon chopped fresh flat-leaf parsley

Zest of 1 lemon

1¼ cups (300 ml) hot water

4 potato rolls

In a large pot, bring 3 quarts (2.8 L) water and the salt to a boil. Add the lobsters, and when the water returns to a boil, cook the lobsters for 5 minutes with the lid on, then immediately take them out of the water and let cool to room temperature. (Do not shock with cold water, as that dulls the flavor.)

While the lobster is cooling, heat the butter in a small 2-quart pot. Once the butter is halfway melted, combine the cornstarch and 1 tablespoon water to make a slurry (see Note on page 120), add it to the butter, and whisk immediately to emulsify. Reduce the heat to the lowest setting to keep warm while you make the breadcrumbs.

Pulse the Ritz cracker crumbs and panko crumbs in a food processor until the Ritz crackers are broken down to the same size as the panko. Add 2 pinches salt, the cayenne, paprika, and granulated garlic and dry-toast the crumb mixture in a sauté pan over medium heat until golden brown, 3 to 4 minutes. Remove the pan from heat, and toss the crumbs with the extra-virgin olive oil, chopped parsley, and lemon zest. Set aside.

Recipe continues

Once the lobster is cool enough to handle, remove the tail and claw meat from the shells by twisting the tail off, followed by the claws. (You can reserve the body in the shell in the freezer for another use, such as lobster stock.) Cut the tail meat into 8 pieces per lobster, and the claw meat into 4 pieces per lobster, and place the meat in the warm butter sauce. Poach in the butter sauce over very low heat, about 6 to 8 minutes, while you prepare the buns.

Butter each roll with about ¼ tablespoon butter per side. (Do not over butter them, as the lobster is very rich.) Lightly toast by placing the buns face down on a grill pan or frying pan over medium heat.

Place the prepared lobster meat in a serving bowl and put one bun on each plate. Serve immediately, passing the lobster meat around the table.

Note: A slurry is a mixture of starch and water used to thicken sauces, stews, and other hot preparations. It is made by combining equal parts cornstarch and water and stirring until a paste forms, then adding the paste to boiling water.

New England–Style Lobster Rolls

Serves 4

½ cup plus 1 teaspoon kosher salt

2 (1¼- to 1½-pound) live Maine lobsters

1 tablespoon chopped fresh flat-leaf parsley

Zest of 1 lemon, plus 2 tablespoons lemon juice

¼ cup (25 g) finely diced celery

10 dashes Tabasco sauce

¼ teaspoon paprika

½ cup (120 ml) mayonnaise

4 potato rolls

2 tablespoons unsalted butter

In a large pot, bring 3 quarts (2.8 liters) water and ½ cup (145 g) of the salt to a boil. Add the lobsters, and when the water returns to a boil, cook the lobsters with the lid on until they are completely cooked through, about 6 minutes. Remove the lobsters to a cookie sheet and place in the refrigerator to cool. (Do not shock with cold water, as that dulls the flavor.)

Once the lobsters are cool enough to handle, remove the tail and claw meat from the shells by twisting the tail off, followed by the claws. (You can reserve the body in the shell in the freezer for another use, such as lobster stock.) Cut the tail meat into 8 pieces per lobster, and claw meat into 4 pieces per lobster. Chop the picked meat into ½-inch (12 mm) pieces, add it to a mixing bowl with the parsley, lemon zest and juice, Tabasco, remaining 1 teaspoon salt, paprika, and mayonnaise and toss to combine. Chill in the refrigerator while you prepare the buns.

Butter each bun with about ¼ tablespoon butter per side. (Do not over butter as the lobster will be very rich.) Lightly toast by placing the buns face down on a grill pan or frying pan over medium heat.

Place the prepared lobster meat in a serving bowl and put 1 bun on each plate. Serve immediately, passing the lobster meat around the table.

CHAPTER 6

The Meat

One of the things I love about cooking meat is the inherent conviviality: I associate meat dishes with get-togethers, whether that means a special occasion or just a big family meal. Eating meat should always feel like an event, and while I'm not suggesting it should be reserved solely for holidays and birthdays, I do think it warrants a kind of welcoming, hospitality-driven treatment that results in dishes meant for sharing. All of the meat dishes in this chapter—which include beef, pork, and lamb—are geared to be crowd-pleasing, and many of them, such as Leg of Lamb on page 142 and the Prime Rib with Parmigiano-Reggiano Popovers on page 132, have fun presentations that are great for gatherings. (I'm the only person in my family who eats pork, but I love it, so whenever I want to make the Roasted Pork Shoulder on page 129, I know it's time to have some people over.)

BISTECCA ALLA FIORENTINA

Bistecca alla Fiorentina is a traditional Florentine recipe, a very simple preparation designed to showcase a really great piece of meat. (In Tuscany, it is often made with meat from Chianina cattle, a local species known to be especially flavorful.) Most people leave the meat out at room temperature to temper for at least an hour before cooking, but I'm not sure I agree with that logic. If done properly, the basting that you do in the pan will help ensure that all of the meat cooks evenly. Feel free to give it a try my way, especially if you are short on time; everything else in this beautiful, hearty dish comes together very quickly.

Serves 4 to 6

4 sprigs fresh thyme

4 sprigs fresh rosemary

Kosher salt

2 (2-pound/910 g) porterhouse or T-bone steaks, about 1½ to 2 inches (4 to 5 cm) thick

¼ cup (60 ml) extra-virgin olive oil

4 tablespoons (½ stick/55 g) unsalted butter

10 leaves fresh sage

6 to 8 cloves garlic, peeled and cracked

4 to 6 lemon wedges

Special equipment: An instant-read thermometer (optional)

COMBINE THE THYME and rosemary in a sachet or piece of cheesecloth tied with kitchen twine.

Liberally sprinkle salt on both sides of the steak. In a large cast-iron pan, heat the oil over high heat. When you see the oil is starting to smoke a little, reduce the heat to medium-high, add the steak, and let it sear on one side for 4 to 6 minutes.

Turn the steak over, then add the butter, herb sachet, sage, and garlic to the pan and baste the meat with a spoon. (The milk solids in the butter will help steam the meat.) Continue basting for 4 to 5 minutes, and then add the lemon wedges to the pan. (You may need to adjust your cooking time depending on the thickness of your steaks and the desired temperature of the meat. To check the temperature, insert an instant read thermometer into the meat horizontally, and look for 130°F to 135°F [54°C to 57°C] for medium rare, 140°F to 145°F [60°C to 63°C] for medium.)

Once the steaks are cooked to your desired temperature, remove them from the pan and place on a wire rack set over a baking sheet, then pour the pan juices over the meat. Allow to rest for 5 minutes before serving.

Cut around the bone of each steak to release the meat and place the bones on a serving plate. Slice the meat at a 30- to 45-degree angle and place the sliced meat on the serving plate, arranging it around the bones. Garnish with the browned herbs and the lemon wedges from the pan.

PORK SCHNITZEL

In 1992, I left the States for an internship not in Italy, but in Germany, at the Hotel Bayerischer Hof in Munich. I knew nothing about Germany or German cooking, but the internship paid, and I figured it was closer to Italy than New York was. It was a challenging—and fascinating—time to be in Germany (the Berlin Wall had come down just two years before), and the restaurant kitchen was a microcosm of the era, a real melting pot of tensions and grievances and the uneasiness of change. (Not that there weren't moments of levity—like the time Michael Jackson came in to eat and we had to figure out what to cook for his pet monkey.) It was an eye-opening experience, both culturally and culinarily, for me—the food I was introduced to there wasn't the food I had dreamed of cooking, but it had soul and lacked pretention, which appealed to me. Plus, there was schnitzel.

I'm a big fan of meat cutlets of any kind, and schnitzel is no exception. Personally, I like the texture of cornstarch more than flour, so that's what I dredge my schnitzel in. This recipe also works with chicken; when I do that, I use the meat of skinless, boneless chicken thighs, which I think have so much more flavor than chicken breasts.

Serves 6

3 cups (240 g) panko

3 tablespoons finely chopped fresh flat-leaf parsley, plus 10 whole leaves

2 tablespoons finely chopped fresh oregano

¼ cup (25 g) finely grated Parmigiano-Reggiano cheese

6 (7-ounce/200 g) pork loins

4 large eggs

1 to 2 teaspoons finely chopped Calabrian chile

1 cup (130 g) cornstarch

Kosher salt

¼ to ½ cup (60 to 120 ml) extra-virgin olive oil

2 to 3 tablespoons unsalted butter

12 cloves garlic, peeled and smashed

6 sprigs rosemary

6 slices lemon, plus lemon wedges for serving

12 fresh basil leaves, torn

Spaetzle (page 159), or grain of your choice, for serving

Special equipment: Meat mallet

Recipe continues

COMBINE THE PANKO, chopped parsley, chopped oregano, and cheese in a bowl and set aside. If your pork loins are on the bone, remove the loins from the bones. Then remove and discard the silver skin.

Place each loin between two pieces of plastic wrap and, using the spiky side of a meat mallet, pound out the meat firmly but gently, on both sides, rotating the meat as you go, until each loin is about ⅜ inch (1 cm) thick.

Put the eggs and the Calabrian chile in a bowl that will be large enough to dip each loin into and mix well with a fork. Spread the cornstarch on a baking sheet and spread the panko mixture on a second baking sheet.

Sprinkle salt on both sides of each pork loin, then place one piece of meat in the cornstarch, coating both sides. Shake off the excess starch.

Dip the loin into the egg mixture, making sure all the cornstarch is covered by the beaten egg, then shake off the excess liquid. Place the loin on the breadcrumb mix and cover the top with more crumbs, then, using the palm of your hands, push the panko mixture deeper into the loin with a fair amount of force. (If you place the breadcrumbs too lightly, they will fall off during frying.) Repeat with the remaining 4 loins.

Line a cookie sheet with paper towels and set near the stove. In a pan, add enough of the oil to go about halfway up the pounded meat and heat over medium. Place two of the breaded pork loins into the pan. Fry for 4 to 6 minutes, then flip to cook the schnitzel on the other side. (The cooked side should be golden brown when you turn it over.) Add about 1 tablespoon butter and some of the smashed garlic, parsley leaves, rosemary sprigs, lemon slices, and basil leaves and sauté. Once the schnitzel is golden brown on both sides, another 2 minutes, remove from the pan and place on the paper towel–lined cookie sheet, and place the aromatics on top of the schnitzel. Discard the cooked oil and herbs then repeat until all the schnitzels have been fried.

Serve immediately with spaetzle and lemon wedges.

ROASTED PORK SHOULDER

I've worked with a lot of Puerto Ricans over the years, and through them, I have been introduced to *pernil*, an absolutely delicious roasted pork dish that is full of flavor, thanks to an overnight marinade and a long, slow cooking process that caramelizes the outside of the roast with lots of spices while leaving the inside juicy and tender. While I wouldn't call this recipe a *pernil* by any means, it was inspired by my desire to achieve that soulful, satisfying depth of flavor.

Prep Note: The pork must rest in the marinade for a minimum of 1 day before it is ready to cook.

Serves 10 to 12

1 (10-pound/4.5 kg) pork shoulder blade roast (fresh pork butt), bone in

1 recipe Marinade (see below)

Special equipment: An instant-read thermometer

REMOVE THE PORK from its packaging and dab it dry with paper towels. Place the meat on a roasting pan and spoon the marinade on top of the pork. Keep the pork in the refrigerator uncovered for 24 hours.

The next day, preheat the oven to 275°F (135°C).

Remove the pork from the refrigerator, trying to keep any herbs and spices that have clung to the outside intact. Roast in the preheated oven for 3½ hours.

Turn the oven up to 325°F (165°C) and roast for 30 minutes, to allow the outside to take on some color.

Loosely cover the top of the roast with foil and roast for another 1 hour 15 minutes, or until an instant-read thermometer inserted near the bone registers 160°F (70°C).

Remove the roast to a wooden cutting block and let it rest for 20 minutes before slicing the meat. Serve immediately.

Marinade

Makes about 3 cups (720 ml)

1 cup (50 g) loosely packed fresh flat-leaf parsley leaves and stems

1 cup (40 g) loosely packed fresh cilantro leaves and stems

1 cup (40 g) loosely packed fresh basil leaves and stems

5 green onions, cut into 1-inch (2.5 cm) pieces

¼ cup fresh oregano

⅓ cup garlic

1 medium yellow onion, roughly chopped

1 jalapeño, roughly chopped (remove the seeds if you prefer a dish with less heat)

1 cup (240 ml) extra-virgin olive oil

2 tablespoons kosher salt

1 tablespoon ground cumin

½ cup (120 ml) lemon juice (from about 3 lemons)

Place all the ingredients into a food processor and blend until smooth, 1 to 2 minutes.

PRIME RIB WITH PARMIGIANO-REGGIANO POPOVERS

One of my early cooking jobs was in the banquet hall at the Sheraton Hotel in Waterbury, Connecticut, where one of our signature offerings were these popovers that we served with prime rib. Popovers have a bit of an old-style reputation, but I say, bring them back. They are super impressive, a bit cheffy, but eminently doable, and just a ton of fun to make. (The secret is cooking the popover in the same pan as the prime rib—as in a Yorkshire pudding—so that the popover absorbs the drippings and the spices from the meat glaze.) When you want to pull out all the stops for a special occasion, this is what to make.

Prep Note: This recipe requires at least 2½ hours of cooking time.

Serves 4 to 6

1 (8-pound/3.6 kg) prime rib, bone-in

Kosher salt and freshly ground black pepper

1 tablespoon Beef Spice Mix (recipe follows)

1 cup (240 ml) extra-virgin olive oil, plus 4 to 6 tablespoons (60 to 90 ml) for cooking the popovers

4 large eggs

2 cups (480 ml) milk

2 cups (250 g) all-purpose flour

1½ teaspoons butter, melted

3 tablespoons finely diced fresh chives (optional)

¼ cup (25 g) grated Parmigiano-Reggiano cheese

Special equipment: An instant-read thermometer (optional)

PREHEAT THE OVEN TO 500°F (260°C). Heavily crust the roast with salt and black pepper, then place in a roasting pan. Roast uncovered for 20 minutes at 500°F (260°C), then reduce the heat to 350°F (175°C) and roast for 2 hours 40 minutes (20 minutes per pound), or until the internal temperature reaches 122°F (50°C). Remove from the oven, turn the oven temperature back up to 500°F (260°C), place the roast on a cutting board, and let it rest for 30 to 40 minutes. (The roast will continue to cook while resting, to medium rare.) Let the roasting pan cool with the juices and fat from the meat.

While the roast is in the oven, prepare the beef glaze by stirring together the beef spice mix, olive oil, and 1 teaspoon salt in a bowl. Set aside.

Prepare the popover batter by putting the eggs, milk, flour, 1 tablespoon kosher salt, the melted butter, and chives (if using). Mix to combine and set aside.

Once the roasting pan is cool enough to handle, discard half of the fat, then add 4 to 6 tablespoons (60 to 90 ml) olive oil (enough to cover the bottom of the pan). Place the roasting pan back in the oven to heat the oil. When it starts to smoke, remove from the oven and carefully pour the popover batter into the roasting pan. Bake for 20 minutes, then turn down the temperature to 250°F (120°C), and bake for another 20 minutes. Sprinkle the grated cheese on top, and return to the oven for an additional 5 minutes. (This will dry the popovers out a little, and prevent them from collapsing.)

While the popovers are finishing in the oven, brush the beef glaze all over the roast, then remove the bones and slice. Remove the popovers from the oven and serve immediately from the pan with the meat.

Beef Spice Mix

Makes 3 tablespoons (55 g)

1½ teaspoons whole allspice berries

1½ teaspoons cumin seeds

1½ teaspoons yellow mustard seeds

¾ teaspoon whole Szechuan peppercorns

½ teaspoon crushed red pepper

4 teaspoons sweet smoked paprika

Leaves of 2 sprigs fresh rosemary

In a small sauté pan over medium heat, toast the all-spice, cumin seeds, mustard seeds, Szechuan pepper-corns, and red pepper flakes, stirring occasionally, until fragrant, 2 to 3 minutes.

Remove from heat and add the paprika and the rose-mary leaves. Let cool slightly before grinding the spice mixture finely in a spice grinder. Store in an airtight container for up to 1 month.

BRAISED SHORT RIBS, TWO WAYS

In the pantheon of big flavors, there's a subtle distinction between "rich" and "rustic." Both connote food that is deeply satiating, but whereas rich dishes are more elaborate and over-the-top, rustic dishes—which I tend to prefer—get their depth from being soulful and immensely crave-able. They are the kind of dishes that, when you taste them, you immediately think, "I need to have more." Short ribs also have a special place in my heart and my repertoire because a braised short ribs appetizer was the first dish that Ruth Reichl called out in her review of Chianti in 1994, the review that put me on the map and convinced me that my cooking was really speaking to people.

These two short rib preparations fit squarely into the rustic category: They're not fancy, but man, they are good. The version with risotto falls more on the side of elevated comfort food, while the fregola option is more bracing because of the pickled Fresnos. Short ribs are fatty, so they need a nice acidic flavor in the braise; for me, red wine isn't strong enough to cut them, so I also include red wine vinegar in my braising liquid. If you have any ribs leftover, use them in the Grilled Cheese with Braised Short Ribs on page 172. (Don't forget to save the braising liquid.)

Note: If you can find them, try substituting beef cheeks for the short ribs in the recipe below; you can cook them exactly the same way, but I find that beef cheeks are more flavorful than short ribs, due to the gelatin content.

Braised Short Ribs

Serves 6 to 8, with either the risotto or fregola

5 pounds (2.3 kg) bone-in beef short ribs, trimmed of fat (especially around the bones)

Kosher salt

¼ cup (60 ml) extra-virgin olive oil

½ cup (60 g) garlic cloves, peeled

3 large onions, chopped

2 medium carrots, peeled and chopped

4 stalks celery, chopped

1 sprig rosemary

4 sprigs thyme

1 cup (240 ml) dry red wine

¾ cup (180 ml) red wine vinegar

1 (14-ounce/400 g) can crushed tomatoes (or whole peeled tomatoes, hand-crushed)

Brown or roasted chicken stock, as needed (see Special Ingredients on page 23)

Preheat the oven to 400°F (205°C).

In a large braising pan, lightly season the trimmed short ribs with salt and sear them on both sides until golden brown, 10 to 12 minutes. Set aside.

Heat the olive oil in a large sauté pan set over medium-high heat, then add the garlic, mirepoix (onion, carrot, celery), rosemary, and thyme. Cook until the vegetables are well caramelized, 12 to 15 minutes. Deglaze with the red wine and vinegar, scraping up the browned bits on the bottom of the pan, then cook for about 6 minutes, until the mixture is reduced by half. Add the tomatoes and cook until reduced by one-quarter, about 6 minutes. Add the ribs and pour in the brown chicken stock to cover them. Bring to a boil, then reduce to a simmer, cover the pan with aluminum foil, and place in the preheated oven. Cook for about 2½ hours. (The ribs are done when you're able to pull away some of the meat with a fork with a little resistance, especially where the meat and bone touch.) Remove the ribs from the pan and set aside to cool.

Strain the sauce through a fine-mesh strainer and discard the solids. Continue to reduce the sauce on the stovetop until the gelatins have added enough body to the sauce that it will coat the back of a spoon. Cool and reserve, skimming off any residual fat.

When the ribs have cooled entirely, break the meat into ¼-inch pieces with a fork, discarding the bone. Return the short rib pieces to the sauté pan with the sauce and keep warm over low heat while you prepare the risotto or fregola. The short ribs can also be made ahead, cooled, and stored covered in the refrigerator for up to 6 to 7 days.

Recipe continues

The Meat

137

Braised Short Rib Risotto with Caramelized Onions

Serves 6 to 8

1 recipe Braised Short Ribs (page 137)

3 cups (570 g) vialone nano rice (see headnote, page 152)

¼ cup (60 ml) extra-virgin olive oil

5 tablespoons (70 g) unsalted butter

Kosher salt

1½ cups (360 ml) dry, crisp white wine

9 cups (2.1 liters) chicken and beef stock combined (you can use all of one or the other, but I prefer the flavor profile of the mix)

1 cup (240 g) Caramelized Onion Purée (recipe follows)

½ cup (50 g) finely grated Parmigiano-Reggiano cheese

In pot set over low heat, warm the short ribs in their liquid while you prepare the risotto.

In a large heavy-bottomed pot over medium-high heat, toast the rice with the olive oil, 1 tablespoon of the butter, and some salt for 6 to 8 minutes, stirring constantly with a wooden spoon. Pour in the wine and cook, stirring constantly, until most of the wine has been absorbed by the rice or has evaporated, 4 to 6 minutes.

Increase the heat to high, then add about 1 cup (240 ml) of the stock to the rice and continue to stir, adding stock gradually, 1 cup (240 ml) at a time, as the liquid is absorbed and you see starch released into the pot. Cook until the rice is al dente, about 18 to 22 minutes total.

When the rice is about halfway cooked, add the caramelized onion purée. Then add the remaining 4 tablespoons (½ stick/55 g) butter and the cheese and stir until just combined. Taste and adjust the seasoning with salt, and place in serving bowl. Pour braising liquid over to taste, then add short ribs. (You may have additional short ribs and braising liquid; see headnote.) Serve immediately.

Caramelized Onion Purée

Note: Though the risotto recipe only calls for half of this yield, you need this volume of onions to achieve the deep caramelization that is integral to their flavor. They are so good that you probably won't have a hard time finding another use for them, but they can also be frozen (up to 2 months) until the next time you make this risotto.

Makes 2 cups (480 g)

¼ cup (60 ml) extra-virgin olive oil

12 cups (1.3 kg) thinly sliced red and yellow onions (from about 3 pounds [1.4 kg], or 5 to 6 onions)

2 tablespoons kosher salt

Heat the oil in a thick, wide-bottomed stainless-steel pan set over medium heat. Add the onions and salt and cook, stirring occasionally with a wooden spoon (about every 10 or 15 minutes), as the liquid from the onions is released and evaporated. When the onions start taking on some golden-brown color, after about 40 minutes, reduce the temperature to medium-low then continue to stir with a wooden spoon. Keep an eye on the pan to make sure the onions do not burn; you can reduce the heat further or add a little water to the pan if they're cooking too quickly on the bottom.

When you start to see some caramelization on the bottom of the pan, reduce the heat to its lowest setting, cover the pan with a lid, and cook for 3 hours, stirring occasionally with a wooden spoon to keep the onions from burning, until they are a deep brown color and have a nice caramelized aroma. (There's a fine line between caramelization and burning, so keep an eye on them, especially towards the end of cooking.) Remove the pan from heat, pour the onions into a food processor, and purée until smooth.

Recipe continues

Braised Short Ribs with Fregola

Serves 6 to 8

Kosher salt

4 cups (720 g) fregola

1 recipe Braised Short Ribs (page 137)

1 cup (100 g) grated Parmigiano-Reggiano cheese, plus additional thinly shaved slices for garnish

4 tablespoons (½ stick/55 g) unsalted butter

Pickled Fresno Chiles (page 14), sliced

Bring a large pot of salted water to a boil, then add the fregola. While the fregola is cooking, warm the short rib slices in the braising liquid over low heat.

Cook the fregola until al dente, about 8 minutes. Drain, place in a serving dish, toss with the grated cheese and butter, then place the warmed short ribs on top. Garnish as desired with Fresno slices and shaved Parmigiano-Reggiano and serve immediately.

DIJON AND DEMI-GLACE GLAZED LEG OF LAMB WITH LEMON-HERB CRUST

Kick your Easter brunch up a few notches with this leg of lamb. Springy and beautiful—after glazing the meat, I add lemon zest, parsley, and chives to the exterior—this dish tastes as good as it looks. That, plus the pop of the citrus and herb, is all the meat needs.

Serves 10 to 12

1 (8-pound/3.6 kg) leg of lamb, bone-in and netted

Kosher salt

1 cup (240 ml) More Than Gourmet brand roasted chicken demi-glace (see Special Ingredients on page 23)

1 cup (240 ml) Dijon mustard

1 teaspoon garlic, minced

1 teaspoon finely chopped fresh rosemary

2 teaspoons finely chopped fresh thyme

2 tablespoons red wine vinegar

1 teaspoon finely chopped fresh chives

1 teaspoon finely chopped fresh flat-leaf parsley

Zest of 1 lemon

REMOVE THE NETTING from the leg of lamb and leave the leg uncovered on a baking sheet in the refrigerator overnight to dry out the skin.

The next day, preheat the oven to 275°F (135°C). Heavily salt the lamb leg and place it in a roasting pan. Cook for 2 hours (15 minutes for every pound of meat).

While the lamb is in the oven, make the glaze: Combine the chicken demi-glace, mustard, 2 cups water (480 ml), garlic, rosemary, thyme, and red wine vinegar in a saucepan and reduce by about one-quarter (to yield about 3 cups [720 ml]).

After 2 hours, raise the oven temperature to 550°F (290°C) and continue to cook the lamb for 15 minutes, until there is a nice sear on the skin.

Take the leg out of the oven, reduce the temperature to 375°F (190°C), then brush the glaze over the meat. Return the leg to the oven, bake for 5 minutes, then repeat the glazing process three more times.

Place the leg of lamb on a wooden board, and sprinkle the chopped chives, parsley, and lemon zest over the top. Let the leg rest for 6 to 8 minutes before carving.

CHAPTER 7

Vegetables *and* Legumes

My Italian grandfather had an incredible garden in the Bunker Hill neighborhood of Waterbury, which supplied many of the vegetables and beans my family ate when I was growing up. He was my introduction to a world of vegetables that stretched far beyond what was available in grocery stores at the time: fennel, zucchini blossoms, borlotti beans, and so much basil. To this day, when I smell basil, I think of my grandfather and how, when standing in his garden, you'd be enveloped by the scent of basil whenever the wind blew.

My grandfather's devotion to his various crops made a huge impression on me and is something I still think about today. It introduced me to the concepts of seasonality and relying on what you grow as the backbone of a meal. He made me pay attention to vegetables, and showed me that good produce, lovingly tended, was just as worthy as meat. While I certainly don't have the time or patience (or space) for a garden like his, I do try to channel his reverence for vegetables and beans into my cooking.

CARAMELIZED ENDIVES WITH LEEKS AND ONIONS

If you've never had cooked endive before, you're in for a treat. Its signature bitterness—which is what puts some people off of eating endive raw—takes on a really deep, interesting sweet note when caramelized. In my restaurants, I've served this warm, as a side with meat or fish, but it's also delicious on its own, warm or room temperature, topped with a little Salsa Verde (page 24). It's super simple—the cooking could not be more straightforward—but trust me, this is an incredibly rewarding dish to have in your repertoire.

Serves 4 as a side

4 heads endive

6 medium leeks, trimmed, white and light green parts only

12 tablespoons (90 ml) extra-virgin olive oil, plus additional as needed

6 small onions, thinly sliced

Kosher salt

Flat-leaf parsley leaves, for garnish

CUT THE ENDIVE AND LEEKS crosswise into ½-inch-thick (12 mm) slices. Wash thoroughly, taking care to remove dirt from the inside of the leeks, and pat dry with a paper towel.

Divide the olive oil between two sauté pans, then add the endive to one and the leeks and onions to the other. Add a little salt to both pans, then sauté over medium-high heat, the endive for 10 to 12 minutes, the leeks and the onions for 15 to 18 minutes, until caramelized. (The pans need to be hot enough so that when liquid is released from the vegetables it evaporates immediately, as that will help cook and caramelize the vegetables. If the vegetables look like they might start to burn, you can reduce the heat to medium.) When both vegetables are done cooking, combine them in a serving bowl, garnish with parsley leaves, and serve immediately while warm.

ESCAROLE AND BEANS

One thing I've learned over all my years studying the way Italians cook: There are some things that the *nonne* do that seem counterintuitive, but somehow yield the best results. Case in point: the double-cooked escarole in this dish. You wouldn't think that simply blanching the escarole—which only takes a minute—before it is sautéed would make such a difference, but somehow that step (which is a tried-and-true *nonna* technique) is what brings the flavors of this dish into focus.

Note: You can substitute 2 cups (340 g) of canned beans for the dried beans, but do not use the liquid from the can of beans, as the citric acid will interfere with the cooking. Instead, substitute water or vegetable broth for the bean-cooking liquid.

Serves 4 to 6 as a side dish

¾ cup (140 g) dried cannellini beans, or 2 cups (520 g) canned cannellini beans

Kosher salt

2 heads escarole, halved then cut into thirds to yield 12 pieces

2 cloves garlic, sliced ¼ inch thick

Pinch crushed red pepper

¼ cup (60 ml) extra-virgin olive oil

2 tablespoons roughly chopped fresh flat-leaf parsley

IF USING DRIED BEANS, soak them overnight in 1 quart (960 ml) water. The next morning, drain and rinse thoroughly with cold water. Place the soaked beans in a pot and simmer in unsalted water for 15 to 20 minutes, or until tender. Drain, reserving about ⅔ cup (165 ml) of the cooking liquid.

Bring a large pot of heavily salted water to a boil. (The water should have the salinity of broth.) Blanch the escarole in the boiling water. (This will happen very quickly—remove the leaves from the pot when they've just started to wilt, 2 to 3 minutes.)

In a large sauté pan set over medium heat, cook the garlic cloves and red pepper flakes in the olive oil. When the garlic starts to brown around the edges, add the blanched escarole and the cooked (or canned) beans. Add the reserved bean-cooking water (or ⅔ cup [165 ml] water or broth) to the sauté pan, season with kosher salt, and cook until the oil and the water create a thin emulsion, 4 to 6 minutes. (You can crush some of the beans with the back of a spoon to release more starch.) Remove from heat, stir in the chopped parsley, and serve immediately.

GERMAN POTATO SALAD

When I lived in Germany, one of my favorite things to eat was their potato salad, usually accompanied by some kind of pork product. These days, I am the only pork eater in my house, so I don't get to eat that meal very often, but I still like to make a riff on that salad that pairs the potatoes with crunchy Persian cucumbers. German potato salad is dressed with a mustard vinaigrette, rather than mayonnaise, which gives it a punchy acidity that I think pairs much better with soft, creamy potatoes. (That also makes it a good dish for a summer barbecue, because you don't have to worry about how long you leave it out—although it is best served warm.) Be sure to use Yukon Golds, rather than Idaho spuds, as their moister flesh absorbs the dressing in a more succulent way.

Serves 6 to 8 as a side dish

¼ cup thinly sliced red onion, then halved into crescents

7 tablespoons (75 ml) apple cider vinegar

Kosher salt

3½ pounds (1.6 kg) medium Yukon Gold potatoes (try to use potatoes around the same size, so they cook evenly)

1 Persian cucumber, peeled, seeded, and cut into ⅛-inch-thick slices

½ cup (120 ml) Dijon mustard

½ cup (120 ml) extra-virgin olive oil

1 tablespoon chopped fresh chives

1 tablespoon chopped fresh flat-leaf parsley

PLACE THE RED ONIONS, 2 tablespoons of the vinegar, and a pinch of salt in a bowl. Let the onions steep while you prepare the potatoes.

Wash and scrub the potatoes thoroughly with a brush to remove any dirt. Put them in a large pot, cover with cold water, and add 3 tablespoons salt. Bring the water to a boil then turn down the heat to a low simmer. (You should see small bubbles, but they should not be moving vigorously.) Cook the potatoes for 20 to 25 minutes, or until a potato poked with a paring knife is pierced with no resistance. Drain the potatoes, reserving 1 cup (240 ml) of the cooking liquid.

When cool enough to handle, peel the potatoes and slice them into ½-inch-thick (12 mm) coins. Place the potatoes in a large bowl with the onion slices and the sliced cucumbers. Discard the onion-steeping liquid.

In another bowl, whisk together the mustard, olive oil, and the remaining 5 tablespoons vinegar. Once they have emulsified, very slowly pour in the reserved potato cooking water. (Do not pour too fast or you'll break the emulsion.)

Pour the vinaigrette over the potatoes and toss with a rubber spatula. Add salt to taste, sprinkle with the chopped chives and parsley, and serve warm or at room temperature.

ANY VEGETABLE RISOTTO

This is one of my favorite back-pocket recipes because it can be completely customized to whatever vegetables you have around, including scraps—broccoli and chard stems, in fact, are some of my favorite things to throw in here. I prefer making risotto with a type of Italian rice called vialone nano, which is very starchy and really soaks up liquid, so it results in a creamy finished product, but you can use the more common carnaroli or arborio if you cannot find it. When cooking the rice with the broth, I think it helps to keep in mind that you are trying to create an emulsion—suspending fat in liquid—so add the broth gradually, stirring constantly, and keep a close eye on the level of moisture in the pot.

Serves 6 as a main course, or 8 to 10 as a side dish

½ cup (120 ml) extra-virgin olive oil

5 to 6 cups (700 to 840 g) finely diced mixed vegetables or vegetable scraps of your choice (carrots, chard, broccoli stems, zucchini)

Kosher salt

1½ cups (190 g) finely diced red onion

1 cup (55 g) thinly sliced green onions or spring onions

1 tablespoon unsalted butter

1 tablespoon fresh thyme leaves

1 tablespoon finely chopped fresh oregano

3 cups (570 g) vialone nano rice (or carnaroli or Arborio)

1½ cups (360 ml) dry white wine

9 cups (2.1 liters) hot vegetable or chicken stock

1 cup (100 g) grated Parmigiano-Reggiano cheese

2 tablespoons finely chopped fresh flat-leaf parsley

1 tablespoon finely chopped tarragon

IN A LARGE SAUTÉ PAN, heat ¼ cup (60 ml) of the olive oil over medium-high heat. Add the mixed vegetables with some salt and sweat them, 6 to 8 minutes. Reduce the heat to medium and cook the vegetables until tender, another 8 to 10 minutes. Remove the pan from heat and set aside while you prepare the risotto.

Put the remaining ¼ cup (60 ml) olive oil with some salt in a large heavy-bottomed pan, 6 to 8 inches deep, and sweat the red onions, green onions, thyme, and oregano over medium-low heat for 6 to 8 minutes, until the onions are translucent but have not started to brown. Add the rice and stir continuously as the rice toasts, until the grains are nicely browned, 6 to 8 minutes. Pour in the white wine and continue to stir until most of the wine is absorbed or evaporates, 4 to 6 minutes.

Increase the heat to high and add about 1 cup (240 ml) of the stock, then continue to stir the rice. As the stock is absorbed and evaporates, watch for the release of starch in the pot, then add more stock, stirring constantly, and repeat the process until the rice is al dente—this means the grains are cooked, but still have a little bite to them. (You may not use all the stock.) Remove from heat, then add the reserved mixed vegetables, the cheese, parsley, and tarragon, and stir until the ingredients are incorporated. Serve immediately.

ROSEMARY LENTILS

This is my stalwart plant-based dish—I've had it on the menu at practically every one of my restaurants since the beginning, and it's been a hit with everyone from carnivores to vegans. I came up with the base of it years ago when I was just playing around with some ingredients at Chianti, and the flavor notes in the combination of lentils, rosemary, and tomato really resonated with me. Ever since, I've served it as a menu item a million different ways, and that versatility translates well to the home: This can be a side for meat or fish (scallops, shrimp, lamb) or a vegetarian main, or you can add some broth and turn it into a hearty, warming soup.

Serves 6 to 8

1 cup (190 g) small green lentils

½ cup (120 ml) extra-virgin olive oil

½ cup (70 g) diced shallots (from about 2 medium shallots)

2 tablespoons chopped garlic

Pinch crushed red pepper

1 tablespoon very finely chopped fresh rosemary

1 (15-ounce/430 g) can puréed tomatoes, preferably San Marzanos

Kosher salt

PLACE THE LENTILS IN A POT with 3 cups (720 ml) water. Bring to a boil then reduce the heat to a simmer and cook until the lentils are tender, about 20 minutes. Drain and set aside.

In a heavy-bottomed pot, heat the oil over medium heat, then add the shallots, garlic, red pepper flakes, and finely chopped rosemary and cook until the shallots are caramelized, 10 to 12 minutes. Add the puréed tomatoes and continue to cook until the sauce thickens. Stir in the lentils and add salt to taste. Serve immediately, or let cool, refrigerate, and reheat.

Optional: For a stronger rosemary flavor, heat a few tablespoons of olive oil and chopped rosemary over medium-low heat for about 2 minutes. Stir the warm rosemary-infused oil into the lentils just before serving.

CREAMY POLENTA WITH STEWED MUSHROOMS

This is the dish that got me married: It's what I made to woo Mel because it's simply irresistible; after Pasta Pomodoro (page 64) and short ribs (page 136), this is the most-requested, most-ordered dish of any menu I've ever written. The richness of the mushrooms combined with the creaminess of the polenta is decadent, eye popping, and almost naughty—like food shouldn't be this good. You'll know you've gotten it right if people swoon when they taste it.

Serves 8 as a side dish or in lieu of a pasta course

7 tablespoons extra-virgin olive oil, plus more as needed

8 medium shallots, halved and thinly sliced lengthwise

Kosher salt

4 cups (300 g) mixed mushrooms, sliced or roughly chopped

4 sprigs thyme

2 (1½-ounce/40 g) containers More Than Gourmet roasted chicken stock combined with 1⅓ cups (315 ml) water (see Special Ingredients on page 23), plus more if needed

1 tablespoon preserved black truffles

Pinch crushed red pepper

1 tablespoon chopped fresh chives

1 recipe Creamy Polenta (see following page)

IN A MEDIUM SAUCEPAN, heat 6 tablespoons (90 ml) of the olive oil over medium heat. Add the shallots, season lightly with salt, and cook, stirring continuously, until the shallots just begin to color, about 4 minutes. Add the mushrooms, thyme, and 1 tablespoon of the olive oil and continue to cook, stirring occasionally, until the mushrooms release their liquid, about 2 minutes. Add the stock, bring to a boil, then reduce the heat to a simmer. Cook, stirring occasionally, until the liquid is reduced by half and has a saucy consistency, 2 to 3 minutes.

Stir in the preserved truffles. If the mixture starts to thicken too much—the mushrooms should be swimming in the sauce—add a few more tablespoons of stock to thin it out a bit. Stir in the red pepper flakes and the chives.

Divide the creamy polenta among four bowls. Ladle the stewed mushrooms over the top and serve immediately.

Recipe continues

Creamy Polenta

Note: It's very important to use coarsely ground cornmeal when making this polenta because it is more savory than finely ground polenta—the dish will be too sweet otherwise. I use an imported Italian polenta brand called Moretti Bramata. If you do not use all of the polenta for the recipe above, store it overnight in the refrigerator and heat it up the next morning with an egg and some grated cheese on top for a quick breakfast.

4 cups (960 ml) heavy cream

4 cups (960 ml) milk

1 tablespoon kosher salt

1 cup (120 g) coarse cornmeal (see headnote)

4 tablespoons (½ stick/55 g) unsalted butter

5 tablespoons (40 g) grated Parmigiano-Reggiano cheese

In a large heavy-bottomed saucepan set over medium-high, heat the heavy cream and milk until scalded, about 5 minutes. Carefully whisk in the kosher salt and continue whisking until the liquid is very frothy, like a cappuccino. While still whisking, slowly pour the polenta into the pot. Continue to whisk until the granules swell, about 8 minutes. At this point, switch to a wooden spoon to stir the polenta. Keep stirring until the polenta has begun to thicken, about 5 minutes.

Reduce the heat to a very low simmer, cover with a tight-fitting lid, and cook, stirring every 10 to 15 minutes, until cooked through and the liquid has reduced, about 1½ hours. (A skin might form on the bottom of the pan, which is fine; do not scrape it.)

Just before serving, raise the heat to medium-high and stir in the butter and the cheese and cook, stirring, until the butter has melted, then take the pot off the heat. The polenta will continue to thicken as it cools, so don't worry if it looks a little thin.

SPAETZLE

Not long ago, I got a DM from someone working one of my TV appearances: "Scott, I'm editing the spaetzle segment, and I gotta tell you, I never seen anyone as excited about any dish, ever, as you are about the spaetzle. My mouth is watering, I'm going to make this tonight." Guilty as charged: I may have Italian heritage by birth, but sometimes I think I must have been German in a past life, because I am crazy passionate about a lot of German foods, especially spaetzle. (My alternate title for this recipe was Little Dumplings of Love.) It's incredibly rustic, superbly textured when cooked right, and simple and satisfying, all at the same time. It pairs well with any braised or roasted meat (try swapping it in for the risotto in the short rib dish on page 138, or for the cavatelli in the Duck Ragù on page 68), the Pork Schnitzel (of course), on page 127, or simply on its own.

Serves 4 to 6 as a side dish

4 cups (500 g) all-purpose flour

1½ teaspoons chopped fresh rosemary

1 tablespoon chopped fresh thyme

½ teaspoon chopped fresh sage

Kosher salt

4 egg yolks from large eggs

2 cups (480 ml) milk

2 tablespoons unsalted butter

2 tablespoons extra-virgin olive oil, plus additional for greasing the pan

Freshly grated Parmigiano-Reggiano cheese, for finishing

DRIZZLE SOME OLIVE OIL onto a baking sheet and set aside.

Mix together the flour, rosemary, thyme, sage, and about a tablespoon of salt in a large bowl. In another bowl, mix together the egg yolks and milk. Gradually add the egg mixture to the flour mixture and mix until the wet ingredients are completely incorporated with the dry ones. (Add a few tablespoons water if the mixture needs more moisture.)

Bring a pot of water to boil. Set a metal grater or a colander over the pot and push the dough through the largest holes of the grater (or sieve) into the boiling water. Remove the dumplings from the water as they float to the surface and place them on the prepared baking sheet. (The oil will prevent the dumplings from clumping.) Reserve about ½ cup (120 ml) of the cooking water.

In a large sauté pan over medium heat, melt the butter and olive oil. When the butter starts to sizzle, add the spaetzle and sauté just until the spaetzle take on some color, then add a few tablespoons of the reserved cooking water and stir to combine. Remove from heat, grate some Parmigiano-Reggiano over the top, and serve immediately.

CHAPTER 8

For the Whole Family

For a chef dad like me, introducing my kids to new foods and flavors is one of the great joys of parenthood. I love watching them develop an interest in the things in the kitchen that I am passionate about, whether it be dishes, techniques, or particular flavors. I also love discovering things about their own personalities through their tastes and watching them evolve into more sophisticated eaters. (Though I do hope that someday, Karya, my picky eater, will broaden her horizons beyond cutlets and plain pasta.)

The recipes in this chapter are our family's greatest hits: our go-to meals that everyone loves (even Karya). They are all easy to pull off in between school and jobs and homework, and they sneak in some extra servings of vegetables here and there. These are also things that we enjoy cooking together. I find that being in the kitchen with the girls is a great bonding experience, and even if they just hang around watching me and asking questions from time to time, I feel like they're let in on one of my favorite things about cooking: expressing love through the language of food.

CHICKEN CUTLETS WITH BURRATA AND MELTED BABY TOMATO SAUCE

My kids are just like me: They are 100 percent all-in on chicken cutlets. The only problem is that it means the three of us really could eat them every day, so the trick is to find ways to prepare them that gives us some variety (and some vegetables). This is a recipe that I did first on the *Today* show, and the feedback we got from viewers was really positive, so I decided to try it for the girls. It's since become a key player in our chicken-cutlet rotation. It's basically a variation on chicken Parmesan, except with better flavor (because of the Melted Baby Tomato Sauce—which I physically have to stop myself from making sometimes because I love it so much—and the milky acidity that the burrata brings). It's also easier to make than chicken Parmesan (because the cutlet doesn't need to return to the oven after the cheese is added).

Serves 4

2 cups (250 g) all-purpose flour

Kosher salt

2 large eggs

4 cups (320 g) panko

¼ cup fresh oregano leaves

½ cup (50 g) grated Parmigiano-Reggiano cheese

1 tablespoon crushed red pepper

4 boneless chicken thighs or breasts, pounded ⅛ to ¼ inch thick with a meat mallet

¼ cup (60 ml) extra-virgin olive oil

4 tablespoons (½ stick/55 g) unsalted butter

4 to 5 sprigs thyme

1 recipe Melted Baby Tomato Sauce (see across)

1 cup (100 g) burrata, at room temperature

Special Equipment: meat mallet

IN A SHALLOW BOWL, combine the flour and a pinch of salt. In a second shallow bowl, beat the eggs with a splash of water and a pinch of salt. In a third shallow bowl, combine the panko, oregano, grated Parmigiano-Reggiano, red pepper flakes, and a pinch of salt. Lightly sprinkle salt over the chicken thighs, then dredge 1 seasoned chicken thigh in the flour, making sure to coat both sides evenly. Shake off excess flour, then dip the thigh into the seasoned egg wash, making sure to coat both sides evenly. Let excess egg mixture drip off then dip the thigh into the panko mixture, pressing down to coat the chicken thoroughly with the breadcrumb mixture on both sides. Set aside and repeat with the rest of the chicken.

Heat the oil in a large sauté pan set over medium heat and add the breaded chicken cutlets, working in batches if necessary. Cook until the breading is golden brown on the bottom, 7 to 9 minutes, then flip and add the butter and thyme to the pan. Cook the second side of the cutlets until golden brown, basting with the browning butter, 3 to 4 minutes. Remove the cutlets to a paper towel–lined plate and lightly sprinkle salt over each one. Repeat until all the cutlets have been fried.

Divide the cutlets among 4 dinner plates. Spoon melted baby tomato sauce over the top, then add a few spoonfuls of burrata on top of the tomatoes. Season with additional salt to taste and serve immediately.

Melted Baby Tomato Sauce

Makes about 3½ cups (840 ml)

2 tablespoons extra-virgin olive oil

1 tablespoon thinly sliced garlic

½ tablespoon chopped fresh oregano

½ teaspoon crushed red pepper

4 cups (580 g) mixed cherry tomatoes, cut in half

Kosher salt

1 tablespoon chopped fresh basil leaves

In a sauté pan, heat the oil slightly over low heat. Add the garlic slices, oregano, and red pepper flakes and sauté for 30 seconds. Before the garlic has taken on any color, add the cherry tomatoes to the pan, turn the heat up to medium-high, season with a pinch of salt, and continue to sauté as the tomatoes release their juices. Once the juices and the pectin from the tomatoes have combined with the oil and have started to form a nice sauce (about 8 to 10 minutes), stir in the basil. Remove from heat and adjust the seasoning with salt. Serve immediately, or store in an airtight container in the refrigerator for 4 to 5 days, until ready to use.

CHICKEN CUTLET SANDWICH WITH RADICCHIO SLAW AND PICKLED FRESNOS

I don't really have an absolute favorite food, but if I had to choose one thing to eat for the rest of my life, it would be my mother's chicken cutlets. It's well-documented in this book that my girls and I are huge fans of chicken cutlets, so I couldn't resist including one more iteration that we all love: a sandwich that pairs the cutlets with the bright crunch of radicchio slaw and a kick of pickled Fresno chiles.

Makes 4 sandwiches

2 cups (250 g) all-purpose flour

Kosher salt

2 large eggs

2 cups (160 g) panko

¼ cup (7 g) chopped fresh oregano leaves

½ cup (50 g) grated Parmigiano-Reggiano cheese

1 teaspoon crushed red pepper

4 chicken thighs or breasts, pounded ⅛ to ¼ inch thick with a meat mallet

¼ cup (60 ml) extra-virgin olive oil

4 potato buns

4 leaves Bibb or Boston lettuce

4 thick slices tomato

½ cup Radicchio Slaw (recipe follows)

Pickled Fresno Chiles (page 14), sliced

PREHEAT THE OVEN to 350°F (175°C).

In a shallow bowl, combine the flour and a pinch of salt. In a second shallow bowl, beat the eggs with a splash of water and a pinch of salt. In a third shallow bowl, combine the panko, oregano, cheese, red pepper flakes, and a pinch of salt. Lightly sprinkle salt over the chicken thighs, then dredge 1 seasoned chicken thigh in the flour, making sure to coat both sides evenly. Shake off excess flour, then dip into the seasoned egg wash, making sure to coat both sides evenly. Let excess egg mixture drip off then dip into panko mixture, pressing down to coat the chicken thoroughly on both sides. Set aside and repeat with the rest of the chicken.

Heat the oil in a large sauté pan set over medium heat and add the breaded chicken cutlets, working in batches if necessary. Once the breading is golden brown on the bottom, about 4 to 5 minutes, flip the cutlets and cook until the other side is browned as well, another 3 to 4 minutes. Place the cutlets on a paper towel–lined plate and lightly sprinkle salt over each one. Repeat until all of the cutlets have been fried.

Slice the potato buns in half, place on a baking sheet in the preheated oven, and toast until golden brown, 4 to 6 minutes.

Remove the buns from the oven and place 1 leaf of lettuce on the bottom of each bun, followed by 1 tomato slice, and 1 cutlet. Spoon a couple tablespoons of radicchio slaw over each cutlet, then add some chile slices to taste, and the top of the bun. Serve immediately.

Radicchio Slaw

½ head napa cabbage

½ head radicchio

2 carrots, peeled and grated on a box grater

¼ cup (60 ml) distilled white vinegar

2 teaspoons kosher salt

1 cup (240 ml) mayonnaise

1 tablespoon prepared horseradish

1 tablespoon sugar

½ teaspoon celery seed

Peel off the outer leaves of the napa cabbage and radic-chio, cut out the core, and julienne.

Combine the cabbage, radicchio, carrots, vinegar, and salt in a large bowl and toss thoroughly to combine. Add the mayonnaise, horseradish, sugar, and celery seed. Mix until all of the ingredients are thoroughly combined, and adjust salt to taste. Serve immediately, or chill in the refrigerator for up to an hour.

CHICKEN FINGER SALAD

This is one of those things that I came up with for when I want to make a meal for the girls that is relatively healthy, and I need to hold out a metaphoric carrot to something they enjoy—chicken fingers—to draw them in. This recipe is also gluten-free and free of dairy. (I like to save my wheat consumption for really good pasta, so I try to cook with non-wheat products elsewhere when I can.) I based the salad around produce my kids love—red bell peppers, cucumber, and avocado—to minimize any potential for pushback. The chicken fingers and salad can be served side-by-side, or the fingers can be placed on top, if you feel like you really need to conceal the veggies.

Serves 4 to 6

1 cup (120 g) gluten-free breadcrumbs

1½ cups (150 g) hand-crushed cornflakes

1 pound 4 ounces (170 g) boneless, skinless chicken thighs, cut lengthwise into 1-inch (2.5 cm) strips

¼ cup (30 g) cornstarch

1½ tablespoons kosher salt, plus additional to taste

2 large eggs

1 tablespoon red wine vinegar

½ cup (120 ml) extra-virgin olive oil, plus additional for frying

½ cup (120 ml) lemon juice (from 3 lemons)

2 large Haas avocados

½ head Bibb lettuce

3 Persian cucumbers, peeled and sliced into ¼-inch-thick discs

1 red bell pepper, seeded and cut into ¾-inch (2 cm) strips

IN A LARGE BOWL, mix the breadcrumbs with the corn flakes. Put the chicken strips in a separate bowl and sprinkle 1 tablespoon of the salt over the top followed by the cornstarch to evenly coat the chicken thighs on both sides.

In a mixing bowl, whisk the eggs, red wine vinegar, ¼ cup (60 ml) water, and the remaining ½ tablespoon salt until the egg mixture is very smooth and everything is thoroughly combined. Line a cookie sheet with paper towels and set aside.

Take a chicken piece and place it in the egg mixture. With your non-dominant hand, remove the chicken from the egg mixture and place it in the breadcrumb mixture, then with your dominant hand, cover the chicken on all sides with the breadcrumbs and push the crumbs into the chicken. Set aside on a plate and repeat with the remaining chicken strips.

When all of the chicken fingers are coated in breadcrumbs, heat about ¼ inch oil in a heavy-bottomed frying pan or a cast-iron skillet. Place chicken strips in the oil, being careful not to crowd the pan. (There should be about an index-finger's width between each strip.) Fry the strips for 6 to 8 minutes per side; if the breading starts turning from golden to brown, reduce the heat. (Otherwise the chicken will be undercooked and the breading will be burnt.) When the fingers are done cooking, place them on the paper towel–lined cookie sheet. Repeat until all fingers have been fried, adding more oil as needed.

In a small bowl, whisk together the extra-virgin olive oil and lemon juice, and salt to taste. Peel and pit the avocados, then cut them into ¾-inch (2 cm) cubes and place them in the bowl of dressing to keep them from browning.

Chop or tear the lettuce into bite-sized chunks and place on a serving platter, add the cucumber and bell peppers, then spoon the dressing with the avocados in it over the top. Serve the chicken and salad immediately, either side by side or with the chicken fingers arranged on top of the salad.

AYLA'S TRUFFLE TAJARIN

Truffles have a lot of significance in our family. When Mel and I were dating, I took her to Piedmont during truffle season for our one-year anniversary. We rented a Jaguar and drove all around the region, eating at Michelin-starred restaurants, drinking at wineries, and gorging ourselves on truffles. Once we were married, truffles were something I frequently cooked when we were home, whenever I could get my hands on them. Once Ayla came along, we brought her into the fold. (Karya not so much, but we're working on it.) I'll never forgot the first time I gave truffles to Ayla, when she was about two, in a buttery pasta dish. She tasted it, her eyes lit up, and her face went straight into the plate. When she came up for air, truffles and butter were smeared all over her face, and she looked at me and said, "Dada, this is DELICIOUS," and I thought, "Man, do I love this kid."

Note: If you can't get your hands on fresh truffles, you could substitute a truffle butter, but I would pass on the truffle oil, which I think has a bit of an artificial flavor.

Serves 4

Kosher salt

20 ounces fresh tajarin pasta (use the Tagliatelle recipe on page 99)

2 cups (450 g) Beurre Monté (page 72)

½ cup (50 g) grated Parmigiano-Reggiano cheese

2 ounces (55 g) fresh black or white truffles

BRING A LARGE POT OF HEAVILY SALTED WATER to a boil. (The water should have the salinity of broth.)

While you wait for the water to boil, gently warm the beurre monté in a saucepan set over low heat.

Add the pasta to the boiling water and cook until just shy of al dente (about 75 percent done), 2 to 3 minutes. Drain, reserving about ⅓ cup (75 ml) of the cooking water. (Do not rinse the pasta.) Add the drained pasta and a few tablespoons of the cooking water to the pan with the buerre monté and cook for another 1½ to 2 minutes, tossing the pasta in the sauce with tongs, or stirring with a wooden spoon. Remove from heat, add the cheese, and season with salt to taste.

Divide the pasta among four bowls and shave the fresh truffles in thin slices over the top, using a truffle slicer or the thinnest setting on a mandolin. Serve immediately.

KARYA'S RICOTTA RAVIOLINI WITH MELTED BABY TOMATO SAUCE

Ayla will try pretty much anything, but Karya is my picky eater, the stereotypical pasta-with-nothing-but-butter-and-cheese kid. This recipe, adapted from one I've had in the restaurants forever, forgoes spice, heat, and weird vegetables and doubles down on the simple flavors of butter, starch, and cheese that all kids love. Karya was also the inspiration for why I toss the raviolini with only the butter and cheese, and then add just a few of those melted tomatoes at the end so they don't overwhelm the other flavors.

Serves 4

8 ounces (225 g) ricotta cheese

2 egg yolks from large eggs

¾ cup (70 g) finely grated Parmigiano-Reggiano cheese, plus more for serving, if desired

Kosher salt and freshly ground white pepper

Semolina flour, for the work surface

1½ pounds Tagliatelle (page 99)

4 tablespoons (½ stick/55 g) unsalted butter

½ recipe cooked tomatoes from Melted Baby Tomato Sauce (page 163), at room temperature

Fresh basil leaves, for garnish

Special equipment: a small ravioli stamp or ravioli mold (optional; see Box)

COMBINE THE RICOTTA, egg yolks, ¼ cup (25 g) of the Parmigiano-Reggiano, and a pinch each of salt and pepper in a bowl and mix thoroughly using a wooden spoon. Set aside.

Liberally flour your work surface with semolina. Roll the dough out, thin enough so that you can see the outline of your hand through it, but not so thin that you see any detail.

Brush the pasta lightly with water, then place dots of filling (about ½ teaspoon each) horizontally at 1-inch (2.5 cm) intervals along one-half of the dough point on the strip. (You can also use a pastry bag to do this; just be sure the opening is big enough to accommodate the pieces of cheese in the filling.) Carefully lift the empty half of the dough and fold the half over the strip with the dots of filling on it, letting it fall loosely over the bottom edge. Gently pat the dough to release any trapped air.

Using a pastry cutter or a small ravioli stamp, cut out tiny squares around each dollop of filling. As you work, transfer the filled pasta to a parchment-lined baking sheet dusted with semolina in a single layer. (An easy way to do this is to hold the baking sheet just below the edge of your work surface and use the cutter to flick and drop the pasta onto the baking sheet. The pasta should glide easily if the surface is well floured.)

When all of the raviolini have been cut and arranged on the baking sheet so they're not touching each other, place the sheet in the freezer. If you're planning to cook the raviolini immediately, freeze them for 40 minutes. The raviolini can also be kept frozen for up to two weeks. (Once the raviolini have been frozen solid, you can remove them from the baking sheet and store in freezer bags or in an airtight container.)

Recipe continues

When ready to cook, bring a large pot of heavily salted water to a boil. (The water should have the salinity of broth.) While you wait for the water to boil, gently warm the melted tomatoes in a small saucepan over low heat. Add the butter to a sauté pan and gently warm it as well. Add the raviolini to the boiling water, and cook until just tender (no more than 2 minutes). Gently drain the raviolini, reserving about ⅓ cup (75 ml) of the cooking water. (Do not rinse.)

Once the butter has mostly melted, remove the pan from the heat, then add the raviolini, a few tablespoons of pasta cooking water, and the remaining ½ cup (50 g) Parmigiano-Reggiano and toss to combine. Divide the raviolini among four shallow bowls. Spoon a few melted tomatoes over the top of each serving, then garnish with basil, oregano, and additional grated Parmigiano-Reggiano, if desired. Serve immediately.

If you enjoy making ravioli at home, you may want to consider purchasing a ravioli mold, a relatively inexpensive tool that cuts down on the cutting and sealing time immensely because you can make twelve (or more) ravioli at a time. These molds are trays with little ravioli-shaped indentations that are serrated around the edges, that usually come with a special rolling pin. After pressing a layer of pasta into the bottom of the mold, you add the filling, then place the second layer of pasta over the top and use the rolling pin to seal and cut the dough. Ravioli molds are easy to find online and in cookware shops.

GRILLED CHEESE WITH BRAISED SHORT RIBS

There are almost always braised short ribs in my freezer. When I make a batch for recipes like the risotto or fregola on pages 138 and 141, I like to make more than I need so I can keep the leftovers on hand for later. (To freeze them, I take the bone off, then chop or shred the meat up a bit, then put the meat back in the sauce and into the freezer.) This big, beautiful sandwich, surrounded by a Parmigiano-Reggiano *frico*, is one of my favorite uses for leftover short ribs. It's gooey and decadent, a ton of fun to eat, and a sure bet that no one will leave the table hungry. Be sure to use challah, because you need a bread substantial enough to support these heavy, gooey fillings, and also because it gets a really nice crust on the exterior when you toast it. This recipe makes three full sandwiches, but that's more than most people can (or should) handle—we cut ours in half. And clearly, you want to serve this with a salad.

Note: Fontal is a cheese very similar to fontina, with the same rust-colored rind, but it's my preference for this recipe because of how well it melts. It's worth trying to seek out, but if you can't find it, regular fontina cheese will do.

Serves 6

2 cups (475 ml) Braised Short Ribs with their braising liquid, meat pulled into pieces about the size of the tip of your thumb (see recipe on page 137)

6 pieces challah bread, sliced ½ inch (12 mm) thick on the bias

6 tablespoons (85 g) unsalted butter, melted

6 slices fontal or fontina cheese (see Note above)

¾ cup (85 g) grated mild Cheddar cheese

6 tablespoons (40 g) grated Parmigiano-Reggiano cheese

PREHEAT THE OVEN to 200°F (90°C).

Add the short ribs and braising liquid to a pot and simmer until the meat is warmed and nicely glazed and the liquid has a thick, gravy-like consistency, 5 to 7 minutes, and then remove from heat.

Brush the tops of the bread with the melted butter, then place two pieces on a flat griddle or a large sauté pan set over medium-low heat (or a griddle pan heated to 325°F [165°C]) for 4 to 5 minutes. Flip the bread, then place a slice of fontal cheese on the top of one slice and ¼ cup (30 g) of Cheddar on the other and cook for 1 minute to melt the cheese. Place 3 to 4 tablespoons of the short rib mixture on the Cheddar cheese side, then flip the fontal cheese slice on top. Watch the sandwich closely, and reduce the heat if the bread starts to brown. Sprinkle 2 tablespoons of Parmigiano-Reggiano on the empty side of the pan, roughly the size and shape of the sandwich. Then, using a spatula, place the sandwich on top of the Parmigiano and cook until the cheese starts to bubble. Remove the sandwich from the pan with a spatula, then flip it onto a baking sheet (so the frico is now on top). Place the finished sandwich in the oven to keep it warm while you prepare the next two sandwiches. Serve immediately.

RACK OF LAMB ON A BED OF SPINACH

Rack of lamb is a superfood for my girls. When they come home late from school or are exhausted from karate or swimming, this is what I make to perk them up. This might sound strange for anyone who has never cooked a rack of lamb at home before, but this is actually a great go-to for when you need to put together a meal quickly because it doesn't require many ingredients or much prep, and the actual cook time (15 minutes per pound of meat) isn't crazy. While I have given instructions for taking the temperature of the meat here, I don't even do that myself because that 15-minute-per-pound rule works every time.

Serves 4

2 racks of lamb, frenched

Kosher salt and freshly ground black pepper

6 cloves garlic, peeled and lightly crushed

1 stalk fresh basil

Drizzle of extra-virgin olive oil

½ cup (120 ml) balsamic vinegar

1 pound (455 g) spinach leaves

Special equipment: An instant-read thermometer (optional)

PREHEAT THE OVEN to 425°F (220°C).

If the lamb racks have fat caps on them, score to just above the meat so that the fat can release during cooking and the meat cooks evenly. Liberally salt the lamb and crack fresh black pepper over the racks to taste.

Sear the racks fat side down in a large cast-iron skillet (or another large ovenproof pan) until they become a deep golden color (about 3 to 4 minutes), then stand the rack up so the bones are upright and sear the rest of the meat of the rack (another 2 to 3 minutes). Intertwine the two rack bones to create the shape of a tent, and place the pan in the oven.

When the racks are at about 115°F (45°C), or 5 minutes before the end of your cook time, place the garlic cloves and basil stalk in between the racks, drizzle a little olive oil over the meat, and continue to cook the lamb racks until the temperature reaches 125°F (52°C), or until the end of your cook time. When the lamb reaches 125°F (52°C), remove the racks from the oven, drizzle the vinegar over the meat, then place the racks on a cutting board and let them rest for 5 to 8 minutes, or until the temperature carries over to 130°F (54°C).

While the racks are resting, place the spinach in the sauté pan the lamb was cooked in, with the garlic, basil, balsamic vinegar, and any fat drippings, and set over high heat on the stovetop.

Once the spinach is wilted, about 2 minutes, put the spinach on a baking sheet lined with paper towels to drain the excess water. Then place the spinach on a serving platter and add the cooked garlic and pan drippings on top. Slice the lamb into chops, place them on top of the spinach, then serve immediately while hot.

BRUSSELS SPROUTS WITH CALABRIAN CHILE RELISH

Brussels sprouts and chiles may not sound like a recipe for a kid-friendly side dish, but there's an alchemy in this combination that transforms these "grown-up" ingredients into something irresistible for the whole family. Brussels sprouts, which many kids find too bitter on their own, absorb liquid really well so they actually are a great vehicle for an interesting, flavorful sauce. The sweetness of the caramelized onions and the crunch of the togarashi helps too. As for the chiles, the amount of heat you add is up to you—I rein it in for Karya, but Ayla really goes for spicy foods, so I'll add some extra for her.

Serves 6 as a side dish

2 pounds (910 g) Brussels sprouts, trimmed and cut in half

½ cup (120 ml) extra-virgin olive oil

1½ cups (190 g) finely diced onions

2 tablespoons minced garlic

1 tablespoon minced anchovy, with some of its oil

1 tablespoon drained and roughly chopped capers (not salt-packed)

1 tablespoon fish sauce

¼ cup (60 ml) balsamic vinegar

1 cup (240 ml) warm vegetable broth

1 tablespoon neonata (see Special Ingredients on page 23)

Calabrian chile, to taste

1 tablespoon roughly chopped flat-leaf parsley

1 recipe Togarashi-Inspired Sunflower Spice (page 27)

PREHEAT THE OVEN to 425°F (220°C).

Toss the Brussels sprouts with ¼ cup (60 ml) of the olive oil and place them flat side down on a cookie sheet lined with parchment paper or a silicone mat. Bake until they are brown on top, about 20 minutes.

While the Brussels sprouts are in the oven, heat the remaining ¼ cup (60 ml) olive oil in a large sauté pan over medium-high heat. Add the onions, garlic, anchovy, and capers and cook until lightly caramelized, 4 to 5 minutes. Add the fish sauce, balsamic vinegar, vegetable broth, neonata, and Calabrian chile to taste (if using) and bring the sauce to a boil for 3 minutes.

When the Brussels sprouts have finished cooking, remove the cookie sheet from the oven and add them to the sauce. Stir to coat the sprouts, then remove from heat and stir in the chopped parsley. Transfer to a serving bowl, top with the togarashi spice, and serve right away.

SUNDAY TOMATO SAUCE WITH MEATBALLS

This sauce practically runs through my veins. Every Sunday of my childhood, no matter what time of year or where we were, there was a pot of this simmering somewhere. (And for the record, we call this "sauce," not "gravy" as some families do.) This recipe, which is loosely based on my mom's, has that signature unpretentious, homey quality, but there's also great depth of flavor because of all of the different meats in it and how long they are cooked for. Per tradition, this recipe has a big yield, and I wouldn't recommend cutting it down; it's a big project intended to have big results. You can freeze leftovers for up to 3 months, if you have them, or follow Italian tradition and give them to your neighbors.

Prep Note: The meatball mixture needs to rest in the refrigerator for a minimum of 2 hours before shaping, and then requires about 3 hours of cooking time.

Serves 8 to 10

Meatballs

1 cup (80 g) panko

¾ cup (180 ml) milk

1 pound (455 g) ground veal

1 pound (455 g) ground pork

2 cloves garlic, finely diced or shaved on a micro-plane grater

1½ teaspoons kosher salt

1 teaspoon chopped Calabrian chile

2 tablespoons chopped fresh flat-leaf parsley

2 teaspoons chopped fresh rosemary leaves

½ cup (125 g) ricotta cheese

1 large egg

3 tablespoons grated Parmigiano-Reggiano cheese

Pasta or crusty bread and grated Parmigiano-Reggiano cheese, for serving

Make the meatballs: Soak the panko in the milk for an hour. Press out any extra liquid, then place the soaked panko in a large mixing bowl. Add the ground veal and pork, the garlic, salt, Calabrian chile, parsley, rosemary, ricotta, egg, and cheese and mix well with your hands. Let the mixture rest for 2 hours in the refrigerator, then scoop into meatballs about the size of the palm of your hand (about 2 ounces [55 g] each), shaping them with the palm of your hand. Place the meatballs on a plate and return them to the refrigerator.

Recipe continues

FOR THE TOMATO SAUCE:

2 tablespoons extra-virgin olive oil

Kosher salt

2 pounds (910 g) beef short ribs

1 pound (455 g) lamb shank

8 ounces (225 g) spicy Italian sausage

8 ounces (225 g) sweet Italian sausage

1 medium onion, finely diced

6 cloves garlic, peeled and crushed

3 sprigs fresh oregano or 1 teaspoon dried oregano

1 teaspoon crushed red pepper

3 (24-ounce/680 g) cans crushed tomatoes, preferably San Marzanos

¾ cup (180 g) tomato paste

Rinds of Parmigiano-Reggiano cheese (optional)

Heat the olive oil in a large heavy-bottomed braising pot with a lid set over high heat. Lightly sprinkle salt on the short ribs and lamb shank and place them in the pot, along with the sausages, and sear the meat for 7 to 10 minutes, until nicely browned on all sides. Set aside. (If all the meat does not fit at once, sear the short ribs and the shank together, then take them out and sear the sausages.) Remove the meatballs from the refrigerator, place them in a nonstick pan set over medium heat and sear until golden brown on all sides, 10 to 12 minutes. (You can add a little butter to the pan to help them brown, if you like.) It's okay if the meatballs lose their round shape a little. Set the nonstick pan aside.

Once all the meats have been seared, add the diced onions, crushed garlic cloves, oregano, and red pepper flakes to the pan that the short ribs, lamb, and sausages were cooked in and sweat them until the onions are translucent, about 5 minutes. Stir in the crushed tomatoes and tomato paste, Parmesan rinds, if using, and all the seared meat (including the meatballs) and bring the mixture to a boil. Reduce heat to a simmer, cover, and cook for 3 hours. Stir the sauce very gently every so often throughout the cooking process to prevent the meats from burning on the bottom.

After 3 hours, taste, adjust the seasoning of the sauce for salt, and serve with the pasta of your choice, crusty bread, and freshly grated Parmigiano-Reggiano on top.

ROAST CHICKEN WITH GNOCCHI ALLA ROMANA

I love roast chicken and have worked for years to develop the perfect roasting technique. It isn't hard, but like so many of my favorite recipes, the key is the attention to detail while you cook. Here, one of the most important steps is making sure that the pan you are cooking in is really hot, so that the liquid that the chicken releases evaporates as soon as it hits the surface, which really helps to tenderize the chicken. You could certainly serve this with plain polenta, but I like to go the extra step and pair the chicken with gnocchi alla romana, which are very different from regular potato gnocchi—they're more like a semolina gratin. The smooth, decadent baked semolina combined with tender, juicy meat and a really deep caramelization on the chicken skin makes for a real textural powerhouse of a meal.

Prep note: The seasoned chicken needs to rest in the refrigerator for 24 hours before cooking.

Serves 4 to 6

1 whole chicken, deboned except for the wing

Kosher salt

¼ cup (60 ml) extra-virgin olive oil

More Than Gourmet brand roasted chicken demi-glace (optional; see Special Ingredients on page 23)

1 tablespoon chopped fresh chives

1 recipe Gnocchi alla Romana (recipe follows)

Special equipment: an instant-read thermometer (optional)

WASH THE CHICKEN and pat dry with a paper towel. Cut in half, season lightly with kosher salt all around and inside the cavity as well. Place both halves breast side up on a wire rack set over a baking sheet and allow to air-dry for 24 hours in the refrigerator.

When ready to cook, preheat the oven to 550°F (290°C).

Brush the skin side and flesh side of chicken halves with the oil and season lightly with salt. In a large cast-iron skillet or another ovenproof pan, sear the chicken skin side down on the stovetop until the skin is a nice golden brown. Place the pan in the oven and cook the chicken skin side down until it is about 90 percent done, 8 to 10 minutes (or until an instant-read thermometer stuck into the center of a breast or where the leg and thigh meet reaches 125°F [52°C]).

Remove the pan from the oven, flip so the chicken halves are flesh side up, and glaze the top of the chicken with the demi-glace, if using. Sprinkle the chives over the top. Serve with the gnocchi and a vegetable of your choice.

Recipe continues

Gnocchi alla Romana

2 pints plus 6 tablespoons (1 liter) milk

1 tablespoon kosher salt

1½ cups (270 g) semolina flour

6 tablespoons (75 g) unsalted butter, diced

1 cup (100 g) finely grated Parmigiano-Reggiano cheese

Extra-virgin olive oil

3 egg yolks from large eggs

Pour the milk into a small heavy-bottomed saucepan and add the salt. Scald the milk by carefully heating it over medium-low heat, stirring continuously, until small bubbles form around the edges. Whisk in the semolina and then switch to a wooden spoon and stir vigorously for 5 minutes. Reduce the heat to your stove's lowest setting and cover. Cook for 1 to 1½ hours, stirring intermittently with a wooden spoon to make sure the semolina isn't sticking to the bottom of the pot. Remove the pan from the heat, stir in the butter, cheese, a splash of extra-virgin olive oil, and the egg yolks.

Lightly coat a large baking sheet with olive oil and pour the semolina mixture into the pan. Place a sheet of wax paper on top of semolina mixture and then use a rolling pin to distribute the mixture evenly across the pan. Chill in the refrigerator until firm, about 2 hours. Once firm, remove the wax paper, then cut the semolina into desired shapes, using a knife or cookie cutter. (The gnocchi can be prepared, cut, and stored in the refrigerator for up to 4 days before you plan to cook them.)

When ready to cook, set the oven to broil. Broil the gnocchi on the baking sheet for about 2 minutes. (Though watch to make sure the tops don't burn.)

CAST-IRON SKILLET CHICKEN WITH FINGERLING POTATOES

This is a riff on a dish that was a staple weeknight dinner in my childhood home and now is once again in my own family's household. It's quick, everything cooks in a single pan, and it's a great use for leftover chicken (such as from the Roast Chicken on page 181), or any other odds and ends you might have in the fridge: chunks of sausage, herbs, some vegetables, whatever. Like all great comfort food, it's humble but sneakily delicious—I have never been able to resist the caramelized drippings you get on the bottom of the pan. It's a wonder my cholesterol is what it is.

Serves 4 to 6

3 tablespoons extra-virgin olive oil

3 pounds (1.4 kg) bone-in skin-on chicken cut into pieces and patted dry with a paper towel (from about a 4-pound chicken)

2 tablespoons kosher salt

1 tablespoon black pepper

2 pounds (910 g) fingerling potatoes, chopped into 2-inch (5 cm) oblique cuts (so there are two angled sides)

1 recipe Basil Chimichurri (at right)

Special equipment: An instant-read thermometer (optional)

HEAT THE OLIVE OIL in a large cast-iron skillet set over medium-high heat. Season the chicken with the salt and pepper on both sides and place the chicken pieces skin side down in the skillet. Fill in the pan with the potatoes. (You want the pan really full so that the surface area is completely covered with chicken and potatoes.) Cover with a lid and cook for 8 to 10 minutes, until the chicken has released its juices and everything is golden.

Flip the chicken, cover again, and cook for another 10 minutes, or until the thickest part of the chicken reaches 165°F (74°C). Remove from heat, add dollops of chimichurri on top, and serve immediately.

Basil Chimichurri

Makes 1½ cups (360 ml)

1 cup (40 g) roughly chopped fresh basil

1 cup (50 g) roughly chopped fresh flat-leaf parsley

¼ cup (35 g) finely chopped red onion

1 cup (240 ml) extra-virgin olive oil

2 tablespoons red wine vinegar

2 teaspoons kosher salt

Add all ingredients to a bowl and stir with a fork to combine. The chimichurri is best served immediately, while the herbs are still fresh, but it can be stored, covered, in the refrigerator for up to 1 day.

CHAPTER 9

Detour *to* Turkish Home Cooking

The first time I went to Turkey, I flew there, by myself, to meet Mel, who was at her mom's house in a small town by the beach near Bodrum. What hit me immediately was the heat, the humidity, and how disoriented I felt after nearly twenty hours of travel. (From New York, where I was living at the time, it was a flight to Istanbul, then Istanbul to Bodrum, then a two-hour drive from there.) Whatever ideas about Turkey I had in my head, it was nothing like what I'd imagined. I realized that I had a lot to learn.

The part of Turkey where Mel's family lives is right where the Mediterranean and Aegean Seas meet, so in addition to being absolutely breathtakingly beautiful, there was a truly distinct sense of place that made a big impression on me. Also, everyone—*everyone*—was Turkish, and since at that point I didn't speak a word of Turkish, it quickly became a joke in the family to see me struggling through every interaction. (Fifteen years later, when I show up to the same stores I visited during that first trip, there's still the same cashiers, and they still remember me as the American who needs help with the money.)

What wasn't foreign to me—and where I immediately felt at home—was the table. Whether sitting down for a Turkish breakfast with her family or walking through towns like Ortakent, getting fresh

seafood from the kiosks, and eating it on the beach together, the connection between food and family resonated with me, and ultimately inspired me, after years of trying to make a statement in Italian cooking, to try to learn a new language, so to speak.

Developing the recipes for this chapter was a labor of love in the most literal sense. As much as I love the foods I've been introduced to through Mel and her family, they are not the foods that I know in my bones from childhood, or that I studied in culinary school, or that I've perfected over the years in my restaurants. To develop these recipes, I had to go back and become a bit of a student again, and faithful as I have tried to be to the way Mel's family eats, these are still, necessarily, my spins on food that is very personal to me. In that part of the world, as elsewhere, there are lots of dishes that seem very similar, but you cross a border or a sea and there are a few different ingredients, a different name, a different secret to success. In that vein, this really is my homage to Turkey: my interpretations of my very favorite dishes and meals I've eaten there, which I would never try to pass off as being traditional preparations, but rather loving riffs on the cuisine that seduced me the second time around.

BÖREK, TWO WAYS

The first thing Mel ever cooked for me was a beef *börek*, and I instantly fell for it—the flavor and texture were seductive, a little mysterious, but not totally unfamiliar. It was like eating something from a past life. *Böreks* are often described as savory pies, but I think that's slightly misleading because integral to the preparation and the amazing taste is the layering of the filling (whether meat or vegetable), the egg glaze, and the *yufka* dough. *Yufka* dough is similar to lavash, or a little like a flour tortilla with some flakiness on the surface; in Turkey, you buy it in the market in big sheets, but it's also sold in packages in specialty stores, Middle Eastern markets, or online, and I recommend you seek it out for these recipes. (The same is true for the black cumin seeds.) Traditionally, the dough is brushed liberally with a mixture of eggs, oil, and milk, but a trick I learned from one of Mel's aunts is to substitute yogurt for the milk, and I gotta tell you, I'm never going back. The glaze transforms into a yogurt-y custard when cooked, infusing the filling with tanginess, and coating all of the nooks and crannies of the *yufka*. Trust me—pie has nothing on this.

Beef Börek

Makes 10 squares

¾ cup (180 ml) extra virgin olive oil

1 large onion, finely chopped

Kosher salt and freshly ground black pepper

2 pounds (910 g) ground beef

4 large eggs

1 pint (480 ml) full-fat Greek yogurt

½ cup (120 ml) canola or sunflower oil

1 pound (455 g) yufka dough (see headnote)

2 tablespoons nigella sativa (black cumin seeds)

In a large heavy-bottomed pot, heat ¼ cup (60 ml) of the olive oil over medium heat. Add the onions, season with salt and pepper and cook, stirring frequently, until softened, about 10 minutes. Add the ground beef, season with additional salt and pepper, and cook for another 10 minutes, until the meat is cooked through.

Preheat the oven to 375°F (190°C) and lightly oil a 9-by-13-inch (23 by 33 cm) glass baking dish. In a medium bowl, whisk the eggs with the yogurt and the remaining ½ cup (120 ml) olive oil.

Start building layers in the baking dish: Place one sheet of yufka dough in the bottom of the dish, then generously brush some egg-yogurt mixture on the dough, being sure to thoroughly coat the bottom. (The yufka will drape over the sides of the pan; it's okay if it tears a little bit.) Add another sheet of yufka, brush with a little more of the egg-yogurt mixture, then add half of the cooked meat. Wrap the sides of the top layer of yufka on top of the meat, then generously brush the top with more egg-yogurt mixture (you can pour some of the mixture over the top to make sure the yufka is very well coated). Add the rest of the meat and fold the remaining sides of yufka over the top. (If you want a more uniform crust on the top, you can add one more sheet of yufka on top, trimming it so it fits perfectly in the baking dish.) Pour the rest of the egg-yogurt mixture over the yufka, brush so that the surface is completely coated, then sprinkle with the cumin seeds.

Bake the börek in the preheated oven until it's golden brown on top and sizzling, about 45 minutes. Let rest for about 20 minutes before cutting into squares. Serve at room temperature.

Eggplant Börek

Makes 10 squares

6 tablespoons plus ½ cup (90 plus 120 ml) extra-virgin olive oil, plus more for greasing the pan

1 large onion, coarsely chopped

1 pound (455 g) mild green peppers (such as Anaheim or Cubanelle), seeded and coarsely chopped

Kosher salt and freshly ground black pepper

3 pounds (1.4 kg) small eggplants, peeled and cut into 1-inch (2.5 cm) cubes

1½ pounds (680 g) plum tomatoes, halved, seeded, and finely chopped

2 large eggs

1 pint (480 ml) full-fat Greek yogurt

1 pound (455 g) yufka dough (see headnote)

2 tablespoons nigella sativa (black cumin seeds)

In a large heavy-bottomed pot, heat 6 tablespoons (90 ml) of the olive oil over medium heat. Add the onions, peppers, and a pinch of salt and pepper. Sweat the vegetables for about 10 minutes, stirring constantly. Stir in the eggplant, season again with little bit of salt, let it brown slightly, then add the tomatoes. Reduce heat to medium-low, cover, and cook until the eggplant is soft, about 15 minutes. Transfer the vegetables to a bowl and let cool slightly.

Preheat the oven to 400°F (205°C) and lightly oil a 9-by-13-inch (23 by 33 cm) glass baking dish. In a medium bowl, whisk the eggs with the yogurt and remaining ½ cup (120 ml) olive oil.

Start building layers in the baking dish: Place 1 sheet of yufka dough in the bottom of the dish, then generously brush some egg-yogurt mixture on the dough, being sure to thoroughly coat the bottom. (The yufka will drape over the sides of the pan; it's okay if it tears a little bit.) Add another sheet of yufka, brush with a little more of the egg-yogurt mixture, then add half of the vegetable mixture. Wrap the sides of the top layer of yufka on top of the vegetables, then generously brush with egg-yogurt mixture (you can pour some of the mixture over the top to make sure the yufka is very well coated). Add the rest of the vegetables and fold the remaining sides of yufka over the top. (If you want a more uniform crust on the top, you can add one more sheet of yufka on top, trimming it so it fits perfectly in the baking dish.) Pour the rest of the egg-yogurt mixture over the yufka, brush so that the surface is completely coated, then sprinkle the cumin seeds over the top.

Bake the börek in the preheated oven until it's golden brown on top and sizzling, about 45 minutes. Let rest for about 20 minutes before cutting into squares. Serve at room temperature.

SIGARA BÖREK

Not to be confused with the *böreks* on page 188, these *sigara* are small, bite-sized treats made of *yufka* dough that is filled with feta and pan-fried. (*Sigara* means "cigarette" in Turkish.) When my mother-in-law comes to visit, she'll make a ton of the filling and fry up batches regularly for us to have as snacks or as an antipasto. They are deliciously additive; Karya will eat these by the truckload, which is saying a lot. (She can make a meal—or three—out of them. They are probably her favorite food in the world.)

Makes 30 to 35 pieces

1 (17.6-ounce) package yufka dough (see headnote, page 188)

1 pound (455 g) feta cheese, crumbled

1 egg yolk from a large egg

2 to 3 tablespoons roughly chopped fresh flat-leaf parsley (optional)

1 to 2 cups (240 to 480 ml) safflower or sunflower oil, for frying

Special equipment: kitchen thermometer or infrared thermometer (optional)

GENTLY SEPARATE THE SHEETS OF YUFKA DOUGH, trying not to tear them as you go. Slice the sheets into triangles about 4 inches (10 cm) long on their longest side.

In a bowl, put the crumbled feta cheese, egg yolk, and parsley (if using) and mix until combined.

Fill a small bowl with water for sealing the dough. Scoop 1 to 1½ tablespoons of the cheese mixture onto the long edge of a triangle of yufka dough, then tuck the two end corners toward each other and roll the dough over the filling down to the third tip (so it's wrapped like an egg roll). Dip your index finger into the water and place it on the end of the yufka dough to seal the tip to the body of the sigara. The final shape should be about 3 inches (7.5 cm) long and about ¾ inch (2 cm) thick (like a cigar). Repeat until all of the pieces of dough have been filled.

Heat the oil in a deep sauté pan to about 350°F (175°C). (This is a shallow-fry, so the oil should only reach about a third of the way up the sigaras.) Add a batch of sigaras, making sure there's about an inch (2.5 cm) between pieces, and fry them until they are golden brown on all sides, 3 to 4 minutes per side. Place the cooked sigaras on a paper towel–lined baking sheet to drain excess oil, and repeat until all the sigaras are fried. (If you are not going to fry all of the sigaras at once, you can store them in the freezer in an airtight glass or plastic container in a single layer, or in layers divided by sheets of wax paper.) Serve immediately, while hot.

SPINACH, FETA, AND EGG BREAKFAST PIDE

When we visit Mel's family near Bodrum over the summer, breakfast is one of the biggest highlights of the trip. (And that's saying something, because the Turkish coast has a lot going for it.) A traditional Turkish breakfast in the home is a thing to behold—no matter what day of the week it is, the table is always full of homemade bread (like the *gözleme* on page 200 and the *cevizli kömeç* on page 211), cheeses, meats, vegetables, olives, eggs, and glasses of tea. (Not surprisingly, lunch is more of an afterthought.) But on the occasions we do go out for a bite in the morning, *pide* is the move. The dough is similar to pizza dough, but denser, creating a boat-shaped bread, in which vegetables, feta cheese, and an egg are baked. (*Pide* is Turkish for pita, but this bread doesn't actually have a pocket.) My rendition adds a little ricotta to the feta, to temper its bite. (Though, full disclosure, my mother-in-law gives me the side-eye when she sees me add it.) It's delicious, fortifying, and worth every calorie; the perfect breakfast when you need something hearty to face the day.

Note: The spinach filling can be a little liquidy, so be careful it doesn't drip off the sides when you put it on the pide to bake. Also, if you have a pizza peel, you can use that instead of a parchment-lined baking sheet to transfer the pide into the oven.

Makes 6 pitas

Pide Dough

Makes 6 balls of dough

¾ cup (180 ml) warm water

½ cup (120 ml) warm milk

1 teaspoon sugar

2 teaspoons active dry yeast

2 teaspoons kosher salt

2½ cups (315 g) all-purpose flour

Combine the water and milk in the bowl of a stand mixer fitted with the whisk attachment and begin to whisk. Add the sugar and the yeast then turn the mixer off and let the mixture stand for a few minutes to allow the yeast to activate.

Change to a dough hook attachment, add the salt and flour, and mix for 8 to 10 minutes on medium speed, until the dough is a little soft without sticking to the sides of the bowl during mixing.

Once the dough is kneaded, let it rest for at least 1 hour, or preferably, place in a 1-gallon (3.8 liter) ziptight bag and let it rest in the refrigerator overnight.

After the dough has rested, divide it into 6 pieces (they should weigh about 4 ounces [115 g] each) and fold each ball of dough under itself to create a tight ball. Cover the balls with plastic wrap while you prepare the filling.

Recipe continues

Spinach and Feta Filling

Makes 1½ cups (about 465 g)

2 tablespoons extra-virgin olive oil

8 ounces (225 g) spinach

Pinch crushed red pepper

1½ teaspoons kosher salt

4 tablespoons (60 g) ricotta cheese

1 cup (150 g) feta cheese

In a large sauté pan, heat the olive oil, then add the spinach, red pepper flakes, and salt. Sauté until most of the water from the spinach has evaporated.

Transfer the spinach mixture to a food processor along with the ricotta cheese and blend until smooth. Crumble the feta cheese into the spinach mixture, then pulse to break the feta up into small chunks.

Assembly

1 pide dough ball

2 to 3 tablespoons Spinach and Feta Filling (left)

1 large egg, plus 1 beaten egg for the egg wash

Pul biber (Turkish crushed red pepper; optional; see Special Ingredients on page 23)

Flaky sea salt

Preheat your oven to the highest temperature it will go up to. (Most gas ovens go up to 550°F [290°C]; most electric ovens go up to 500°F [260°C].) Place a pizza stone or large baking sheet in the oven.

Roll out the dough lengthwise on a piece of parchment paper, if you don't own a pizza peel, so it is ⅛ to ¼ inch thick, about 8 to 9 inches long (20 to 23 cm), and 4 inches (10 cm) wide.

Take the corner of the dough that is closest to you and roll it about ¼ inch toward the middle, creating a small triangle. Then continue to fold that corner of dough in the same way, moving up the edge of the dough, pinching as you go, until you get to the top; you will have created a shallow wall on one side. Then do the same thing with the other corner; when you get to the top, fold up the edge of the dough on the opposite side, creating a boat (or diamond) shape, with both sides rolled in and the ends pinched down. Carefully transfer the dough to a parchment-lined cookie sheet. Brush the egg wash over the edge of the dough, then place the spinach filling in the middle. Using a spoon, create a crater in the spinach mixture on which the egg will eventually be placed.

Carefully place the pide in the oven on a pizza stone or cookie sheet. (If you don't have a pizza peel, you can hold the corners of the parchment paper you put under the dough to transfer the bread to the oven.) Crack the eggshell on the side of a small bowl, then gently and swiftly open the egg into the crater in the center of the spinach. Bake for about 10 minutes, until the edges of the dough are golden brown, the yolk is firm in the middle, and the whites of the eggs are cooked through. Remove the pide from the oven, sprinkle with red pepper flakes, if using, and season with flakey sea salt to taste. Serve immediately. (Repeat with the additional dough balls if making multiple pides, or reserve dough and spinach mixture for another time. The spinach will last for up to 2 days refrigerated, the dough up to 5.)

LAHMACUN

This is another entry in the canon of great Turkish flatbreads, and a staple of local street food that is zesty, flavorful, and eaten on the fly. It's sometimes referred to as "Turkish pizza," but *lahmacun* is traditionally topped with minced meat and vegetables, not cheese, and while the cooked shape resembles a pizza, it's often rolled onto itself before it's eaten.

Note: If you have a pizza peel, you can use that instead of parchment paper to transfer the lahmacun into the oven.

Lahmacun Dough

Makes 8 dough balls

1½ cups (360 ml) warm water

1½ teaspoons active dry yeast

3 cups (375 g) all-purpose flour

1 tablespoon extra-olive oil

Topping

Makes 5 cups (1.2 g)

2 pounds (910 g) ground lamb

1 tablespoon kosher salt

2 to 2½ tablespoons Turkish red pepper paste (I use Öncü; see Special Ingredients on page 23)

½ cup (85 g) finely chopped onion

1 tablespoon chopped garlic

2 to 2½ tablespoons tomato paste

2 tablespoons roughly chopped fresh flat-leaf parsley

1 teaspoon pul biber (Turkish crushed red pepper; see Special Ingredients on page 23)

⅓ cup finely chopped Anaheim peppers, or other mild green chile pepper

½ cup (40 g) finely chopped green onions

Recipe continues

Finishing

Semolina flour, for dusting

Chopped fresh flat-leaf parsley

Sliced tomatoes

Thinly sliced onions (soaked in ice water for 10 minutes and drained)

Extra-virgin olive oil, lemon juice, and additional pul biber to taste

Prepare the dough: Combine the warm water with the yeast in the bowl of a stand mixer fitted with a dough hook attachment and whisk until the yeast has dissolved in the water. Add the oil and flour and mix on low speed until the ingredients have come together. Increase the speed to medium and continue to mix until the dough is smooth, about 10 minutes more. Place the dough on a well-floured countertop, cover with a bowl, and let rest for about 30 minutes.

Make the topping: While the dough is resting, prepare the topping by mixing all ingredients together in a bowl.

When the dough has finished resting, preheat oven to its highest setting (500°F to 550°F [260°C to 290°C]). Place a pizza stone or baking sheet in the oven.

Divide the dough into 8 equal pieces, rolling each piece under itself to create tight balls. Cover the balls with plastic wrap.

Place a piece of parchment paper on the countertop and dust it with semolina. Take one dough ball and roll it out 10 to 12 inches wide (25 to 30 cm) and about ¼ inch thick. Take about 8 to 10 tablespoons (120 to 150 g) of the meat mixture and spread it out evenly on top of the dough, leaving about ½ inch (2.5 cm) of the outer rim of the dough bare. (Use more meat mixture if needed in order to completely cover the surface of the dough.)

If you don't have a pizza peel, transfer the lahmacun to the oven by picking up the edges of the parchment and carefully placing it on the hot pizza stone or baking sheet. Bake for about 8 minutes, until the outer edges have taken on a bit of color and the middle of the dough is cooked but not dried up. Remove from the oven and add chopped parsley, tomatoes, and sliced onion to taste. Drizzle with extra-virgin olive oil, a squeeze of lemon, and another pinch of pul biber. Serve immediately, either open-faced or rolled onto itself, as they often do in Turkey.

GÖZLEME

Sitting down for a Turkish breakfast as a family is one of the most special things about the culture for me. As someone who was raised among people who prized abundant family meals, I felt an instant connection to the ritual, and then was blown away by the food that's laid out to start the day: the cheese, the meat, the vegetables, preserves, and of course, my favorite, the breads. The array of Turkish breads is stunning, and they are all delicious, but if I had to choose my favorites, it would be the walnut bread (page 211), and *gözleme*. It's made from a very simple dough that's kneaded, rolled, pressed, then rolled again so that it forms layers inside, similar to how you make a scallion pancake.

Makes 3 pieces gözleme;
serves 3 to 6

1 cup (240 ml) warm water

½ teaspoon active dry yeast

2 cups (250 g) all-purpose flour or bread flour, which will stretch more, plus extra for rolling

3 tablespoons full-fat Greek yogurt

½ teaspoon baking powder

½ teaspoon kosher salt, plus more as needed

1 cup (240 ml) extra-virgin olive oil, plus additional as needed

Kosher salt

1½ tablespoons unsalted butter

COMBINE THE WARM WATER and the yeast in the bowl of a stand mixer with a dough hook attachment. When all of the yeast is dissolved, add the flour, yogurt, baking powder, and salt and mix for 8 to 10 minutes on medium speed until the dough looks soft and very smooth. Transfer the dough to a countertop covered with plastic wrap and let rest for 30 minutes.

Once the dough has rested, divide it into 6 pieces and form tight balls by folding the dough of each piece under itself. Cover the balls with plastic wrap to keep them from drying out.

Dust the countertop with flour. Take 1 ball of dough and roll it out with a rolling pin, dusting with flour as you go so the dough doesn't stick to the counter or the rolling pin. Roll the dough out as thinly as you can without tearing it (about as thin as filo), until the dough is 10 to 12 inches (25 to 30 cm) wide.

Drizzle the dough with olive oil (about 2 tablespoons) and brush it evenly over the top, then lightly sprinkle with salt. Roll out another piece of dough, place it on top of the first piece of dough and repeat the process with the oil and salt. Fold the edges of the dough into the center to create a square shape. Repeat with the remaining dough sheets so you end up with 3 squares of dough, about 5 by 5 inches (12 cm) each.

Place 1 tablespoon olive oil and ½ tablespoon butter in a sauté pan, then add one square of dough. Cover and cook on medium-low heat for 3 to 4 minutes on each side, until golden brown and griddled-looking. Repeat with the remaining squares. Serve immediately, while warm.

MANTI

There's a *manti* place around the corner from where we stay in Bodrum, so whenever we go there, that's our first stop when we get into town. Watching the women prepare them in the back of the shop is intense: The surfaces are covered with tiny squares of dough, and the cooks stand over them methodically placing little dollops of meat on each one, folding each batch into tiny pinwheels, and starting again.

While not hard to make, *manti* (pronounced "manta") are, admittedly, a lot of work—it is time-consuming to cut, fill, and fold such small dumplings—but the results are worth it. Topped with yogurt sauce, spicy melted butter, and dried mint, the flavor is a knockout. (Though you can also omit the spices and sauces, as Karya likes, and serve them plain.)

Makes about 240 manti; serves 4 to 6

FOR THE DOUGH:

4 cups (500 g) all-purpose flour, plus more for shaping the dumplings

4 large eggs

2 teaspoons kosher salt

FOR THE FILLING:

8 ounces (225 g) ground beef

½ medium onion, grated on the medium-sized holes of a box grater or diced

3 tablespoons finely chopped fresh parsley

Kosher salt and black pepper

FOR THE YOGURT SAUCE:

3 cups (720 ml) full-fat Greek yogurt

3 cloves garlic, minced

Pinch kosher salt (optional)

FOR THE BUTTER SAUCE:

¼ cup (½ stick/55 g) unsalted butter

1 tablespoon paprika

2 tablespoons tomato sauce (optional)

2 teaspoons dried mint

leaves

Pul biber (Turkish crushed red pepper; optional; see Special Ingredients on page 23)

PREPARE THE DOUGH: In a bowl, mix together the flour, eggs, salt, and scant ½ cup (120 ml) water. (Only add as much water as you need to prevent the dough from being sticky.) Knead for 2 to 3 minutes, until smooth. Cover the dough and let it sit for 1 hour.

While the dough rests, prepare the filling: Combine the beef, grated onion, chopped parsley, and some salt and black pepper in a bowl and mix well. Set aside.

Once the dough has rested, evenly divide it into 2 or 3 balls. Using a rolling pin or a dowel, roll a ball of dough into a large flat disk, about 1/16 inch (2 mm) thick. Take a sharp knife or a pizza cutter and cut the dough into 1-inch (2.5 cm) squares.

Lightly flour a cookie sheet. Place ½ teaspoon meat mixture in the center of each square. Pull the corners of the squares up to the middle and pinch the seams to enclose the meat filling and create a pinwheel-like shape. Transfer the shaped manti to the prepared cookie sheet. Repeat with the remaining ball(s) of dough and filling. (You can prepare them to this point and store them in the freezer for later use, if you prefer.)

Bring a large pot of heavily salted water to a boil. (The water should have the salinity of broth.) While waiting for the water to boil, make the yogurt sauce by mixing the yogurt with the minced garlic, and a pinch of salt, if desired. Set aside, at room temperature. When the water comes to a boil, carefully drop the manti into the water and cook for 8 to 10 minutes.

While the manti are cooking, in a small pot set over medium heat, melt the butter, then stir in the paprika and tomato sauce (if using). Turn off the heat but keep the pot on the burner so it'll be warm when you pour it over the manti.

When the manti are done cooking (about 3 minutes after they have floated to the top of the pan), drain them, reserving some of the cooking water, if desired. (Some people in Turkey like to add this to their bowls, or eat it separately, like a soup. Either way is delicious!) Divide the dumplings among four to six bowls, top each serving with the yogurt, then drizzle with some butter sauce. Garnish with the dried mint leaves and sprinkle with pul biber flakes if you want more heat.

MENEMEN

This is a specialty of Mel's uncle that he loves to make for us whenever we visit Bodrum. It's basically scrambled eggs with vegetables, but the key is to sweat the vegetables first, so that once the eggs are added, they are really cooking in the vegetables' juices, which creates a richer flavor.

Serves 4 to 6

3 tablespoons extra-virgin olive oil

1 cup (150 g) diced Anaheim pepper or other mild green pepper

¾ cup (95 g) diced yellow or white onion

¾ cup (120 g) diced red bell pepper

1 cup (55 g) thinly sliced green onion

½ teaspoon pul biber (Turkish crushed red pepper; see Special Ingredients on page 23)

Kosher salt

4 cups (720 g) diced tomato

12 large eggs, beaten

1½ tablespoons chopped fresh mint leaves

1½ tablespoons chopped fresh flat-leaf parsley leaves

HEAT THE OLIVE OIL in a large sauté pan set over medium heat, then add the Anaheim peppers, onions, red peppers, green onions, and crushed red pepper. Add a little bit of salt and sweat the vegetables, stirring continuously. Once the vegetables are translucent with slight color, about 6 to 8 minutes, add the tomatoes. Continue to cook until most of the liquid has evaporated, about 5 to 8 minutes. Add the eggs and stir while cooking them to ensure that they cook evenly.

Season with salt to taste and sprinkle with the chopped parsley and mint. Place the eggs on a plate and serve immediately.

YAPRAK SARMA (STUFFED GRAPE LEAVES)

Though often served as a cold mezze in the United States, in Turkey, stuffed grape leaves are served warm, with a dollop of yogurt and lemon wedges on the side. If you've never had one that's freshly made, you're in for a treat: The texture and aroma of the warm, seasoned rice surrounded by an oil-kissed grape leaf is really, really special. This recipe makes enough for a small crowd (though I would not underestimate how addictive they are); leftovers can be kept in the refrigerator for up to 3 days and reheated.

Note: If the grape leaves you buy are jarred, you will need to rinse them in water to remove the brine, then lay them on paper towels to absorb the excess moisture before you use them.

Makes about 40 pieces

1½ cups (360 ml) extra-virgin olive oil

3 medium onions, finely chopped

2 tablespoons tomato paste

1½ cups (270 g) rice of your choice (baldo is traditional in Turkey)

¼ cup (25 g) chopped fresh flat-leaf parsley leaves, plus some stems reserved separately

1½ tablespoons dried mint leaves

1 teaspoon sugar

Kosher salt and black pepper

40 jarred or fresh grape leaves

Lemon wedges and Greek yogurt, for serving (optional)

HEAT 1 CUP (240 ML) OF THE OLIVE OIL in a large sauté pan set over medium heat. Add the onions and sweat them, stirring continuously, just until translucent. Stir in the tomato paste.

Rinse and drain the rice in a fine-mesh sieve and add it to the pan with the onions. Pour in 1 cup (240 ml) water, bring to a boil, then reduce the heat to a simmer and place a lid on top. Once all of the liquid has been absorbed, about 10 to 15 minutes, remove from heat. (The rice will not be fully cooked at this point.) Add the parsley leaves, mint, sugar, and salt and black pepper to taste, and mix well. Leave the lid on the pot to keep the rice warm.

Spread out the grape leaves individually on a flat surface, working in batches if necessary. Arrange 1 tablespoon rice mixture in a straight line across the center of each grape leaf. Fold in the sides, then fold the top over the rice, and roll the leaf toward you into a long thin pencil shape. The perfect stuffed grape leaves aren't too loosely rolled or too tight (if they are rolled too tightly, the rice will burst through the leaves as it expands during cooking). Repeat with the remaining grape leaves and filling.

Once all the leaves are filled and rolled, place some of the parsley stems on the bottom of a pot, add a layer of stuffed grape leaves, then add a few more parsley stems on top. Add another layer of stuffed grape leaves perpendicular to the one below it, and continue layering, alternating between horizontal and vertical layers, with the rest of the stuffed leaves. Add about 2 cups (480 ml) hot water, or enough to cover the stuffed leaves, and some salt, then cover and cook over medium-low heat for 30 to 40 minutes. When most of the water has evaporated, drizzle the remaining ½ cup (120 ml) olive oil over the top (this will provide a nice glaze to the grape leaves). Serve immediately, while warm, topped with a dollop of yogurt and lemon wedges on the side, if desired.

DOLMAS (STUFFED VEGETABLES)

These are a family favorite—both girls absolutely love them. (In fact, similar to the Chicken Finger Salad on page 166, this is a great way to sneak a lot of vegetables into kid-friendly staples like ground beef and rice.) In Turkey, *dolma* can refer to any stuffed vegetable (the word means "stuffing" or "filling" in Turkish), whereas the grape leaves on page 207 are known as *yaprak sarma*, or wrapped leaves.

Serves 4 to 6 as a main course

6 small Cubanelle peppers (about 1 pound/455 g), or other mild green chiles, stemmed, cored, and seeded

3 medium zucchini (about 1½ pounds/680 g), halved crosswise, seedy flesh scooped out

2 teaspoons kosher salt, plus additional to taste

1¼ teaspoons freshly cracked black pepper, plus additional to taste

12 ounces (340 g) ground beef chuck

1 cup (125 g) finely chopped onions

1 cup (180 g) finely chopped tomato

½ cup (90 g) long-grain rice

¼ cup (25 g) finely chopped fresh flat-leaf parsley, plus additional for garnish

2 tablespoons extra-virgin olive oil, plus additional to taste

2 teaspoons fresh thyme leaves

2 tablespoons tomato paste

¾ cup (180 ml) full-fat Greek yogurt

½ teaspoon finely grated garlic

¼ teaspoon dried oregano

Pul biber (Turkish crushed red pepper; see Special Ingredients on page 23), optional

SEASON THE PEPPERS and zucchini inside and out with salt and pepper to taste and arrange them snugly, standing upright, in a saucepan.

In a medium bowl, combine the beef, onion, tomato, rice, parsley, olive oil, thyme, 2 teaspoons salt, and 1 teaspoon black pepper and mix well. Spoon the filling into the peppers and zucchini, filling them until the filling is level with the edge of the vegetable. (The rice will expand when cooking, creating a nice mound on top.)

In a small bowl, whisk the tomato paste into 1 cup (240 ml) water. Pour the tomato mixture around the vegetables and bring to a simmer over moderately low heat. Cover and cook until the vegetables are tender and the filling is cooked through, about 25 minutes.

Put the yogurt in a small bowl and stir in the garlic. Transfer the stuffed vegetables to a platter and drizzle with some of the cooking liquid from the pan. Spoon the yogurt over the top, sprinkle with oregano and pul biber, if desired, and serve.

CEVIZLI KÖMEÇ (WALNUT BREAD)

A staple of the Turkish breakfast table, *cevizli kömeç*, or walnut bread, took some time to grow on me. The bread itself is a little dry, made up of layers of thin dough, like *Gözleme* (page 200) wrapped around the walnuts. But after trying it a few times, I was able to appreciate its subtle but deep texture and flavor, and now I'm so addicted I can't keep it around the house. If you don't have time for a full Turkish breakfast, this walnut bread is delicious on its own, toasted and dipped in a little extra-virgin olive oil.

Makes 1 loaf

3¼ cups (440 g) bread flour, plus additional for dusting the work surface

1 cup (240 ml) full-fat Greek yogurt

½ cup (120 ml) olive oil, plus additional for brushing the dough

1 cup (240 ml) warm water

1 teaspoon kosher salt

2 teaspoons instant dry yeast

2 cups (240 g) coarsely chopped walnuts

Kosher salt

Egg wash (1 egg whisked with 1 tablespoon water)

3 tablespoons nigella sativa (black caraway seeds)

PUT THE BREAD FLOUR, yogurt, olive oil, warm water, salt, and yeast in a bowl and mix with an electric mixer until smooth, about 5 minutes on medium speed. (When handling the dough, the consistency should be soft but not sticky.) Cover the dough with a bowl and let is rest on the counter for 1 hour.

Separate the dough into 8 even portions. Lightly dust your countertop with flour then place 1 portion of dough in the middle and start to roll it out with a rolling pin, sprinkling with additional flour if the dough starts to stick. Roll until the dough is very thin (as thin as a piece of filo dough) and roughly 2 by 2 feet (30 by 30 cm). Repeat with remaining portions of dough.

Take 1 sheet of dough, drizzle a little olive oil over it, then use a pastry brush to evenly coat the dough. Sprinkle ¼ cup (30 g) of the walnuts on the dough, then lightly sprinkle with kosher salt.

Repeat the process with the next piece of dough, layering 1 sheet of dough over another until you've filled and layered all 8 pieces of dough. Then take one side of the dough pile and roll it into itself in a long roll (like rolling up a cinnamon roll). Place the dough in a large round cake pan (about 11 to 12 inches [28 to 30 cm] wide), with the spiral shape facing up. Lightly press down on the spiral to spread out the dough to cover the whole cake pan. Lightly brush the top of the dough with the egg wash and lightly sprinkle the black caraway seeds and some salt on top; let the dough rest at room temperature for about 20 minutes.

Meanwhile, preheat the oven to 350°F (175°C).

Bake until the top is golden brown, 45 to 60 minutes. Remove from the oven and set aside until cool enough to slice. Serve warm or at room temperature. (This bread will last for 3 days, covered, at room temperature.)

CHAPTER 10

Sweets

I'm not a huge dessert person, but I am outnumbered in my family, so when I do make sweets, it's usually for them. That said, you don't have to twist my arm too much to make the *Zwetschgenkuchen* (page 224), since I'll confess that I have a fondness for a little slice of plum cake with my espresso. I keep the Angel Wings (page 214) and biscotti (page 216) around for the same reason—it really enhances the espresso experience to have a sweet bite alongside of it. (Though maybe take that with a grain of salt, since I tend to think most things go well with espresso, given that I drink it so regularly throughout the day.) Other desserts that stand out for me are the Whoopie Pies (page 222), which remind me of childhood visits to Maine, and chocolate soufflé (page 217), which I am powerless to resist if I see it on a menu. And then hands down my favorite dessert—maybe even my favorite recipe in this entire book—is the buttery, nutty hazelnut cake from L'Impero (page 220).

Okay, maybe I am a little bit of a sweets person after all.

ANGEL WINGS

Growing up, as much as I loved family meals themselves, probably my favorite part was after dinner, when we all lingered around the table, enjoying one another's company. The adults would pass around a bottle of Strega, an amaro from Benevento, known as "the city of witches," which is the town in Italy where my mother's family is from. (*Strega* means "witch" in Italian.) There was also coffee, bowls of nuts and nutcrackers scattered around, and always a plate of angel wings and *taralli* in the middle of the table. They weren't dessert per se, but more like little enticements to keep the gathering going, perfect to nibble on or absently swirl around in a cup of espresso during the lively conversation. I don't eat *taralli* anymore, but I still have a soft spot for these angel wings. Sweet, sociable, and universally appealing (who doesn't like fried dough?), these are good at any time of day. When I think of "having coffee" with someone, there are always angel wings in that image.

Makes about 48 wings

1 cup (125 g) all-purpose flour, sifted, plus extra to work the dough if needed

2 large eggs, plus another if needed

¼ cup (50 g) granulated sugar

½ tablespoon vanilla extract

1 tablespoon whiskey

1½ quarts (1.4 liters) vegetable oil, for deep frying

Confectioners' sugar, for dusting

Special equipment: a kitchen thermometer, a pasta roller (both optional), a pastry wheel or pizza cutter

PUT THE FLOUR in a large bowl. In a medium bowl, mix the eggs, sugar, vanilla, and whiskey together. Pour the liquid mixture into the flour and, using a wooden spoon or a mixer, work it into a dough. (The dough should be the consistency of pasta dough. If it is too moist, add a little more flour. If it's very dry, add another egg; if it's slightly dry, add a few tablespoons water.)

Knead the dough for 2 to 3 minutes, then shape it into a tight ball, cover with plastic wrap, and let it rest at room temperature for a least 1 hour.

After the dough has rested, cut it into 4 pieces and cover 3 of the pieces with plastic wrap. Roll out the uncovered piece of dough as thinly as you can, or until it is about ⅛ inch thick. (Alternatively, if you have a pasta roller, roll out the piece of dough thin enough to pass through the pasta roller on the thickest setting. Dust with flour, pass through the pasta roller, then fold the dough in half and repeat until you end up with a rectangular piece of dough that is ⅛ inch thick.)

Lightly dust your work surface with flour and lay the rolled-out dough on top. Using a pastry wheel or pizza cutter, cut the dough into 12 rectangles, approximately 3 to 4 inches (7.5 to 10 cm) long and 2 inches (6 cm) wide.

Using the pastry wheel, cut a small lengthwise slit down the middle of each rectangle of dough. (If you make the opening too big, the dough will fold onto itself while frying.) Pull one end of the dough through the slit so it folds over itself to create a wing shape. (Alternatively, you can just punch the dough in the middle so it looks like a bow tie.) After all of the dough has been shaped into wings, repeat the previous two steps with the remaining dough balls.

Heat the vegetable oil in a heavy-bottomed pot to 350°F (175°C). (There should be about 1 inch (2.5 cm) oil in the bottom of the pan.) Set a paper towel–lined baking sheet nearby. Drop a batch of angel wings in the oil, being careful not to crowd the pan. When the bubbles around each dough strip disappear and you see a golden color around the edges, flip and fry on the other side. Transfer the fried dough to the paper towel–lined baking sheet, and dust with confectioners' sugar while the dough is still warm. Repeat with remaining batches. Serve immediately or keep in an airtight container for up to 6 days.

CHOCOLATE CHIP–PECAN BISCOTTI

This has been my go-to biscotti recipe since my L'Impero days in the early 2000s, despite the fact that the flavors—chocolate chip, oats, and pecan—are not remotely Italian. Biscotti are traditionally baked two times (the word *biscotti* in Italian derives from the Latin term for "twice cooked"), but I like to really underbake them the second time, so they have that signature crispness on the outside, but are still a little soft on the inside. These are not the kind of biscotti that you have to worry about breaking your teeth on.

Makes 20 to 30 cookies

2½ cups (315 g) all-purpose flour, plus additional for the work surfaces

1½ teaspoons baking powder

½ teaspoon kosher salt

½ teaspoon ground cinnamon

½ cup (45 g) old-fashioned rolled oats

½ cup (1 stick/115 g) unsalted butter, softened

1¼ cups (250 g) sugar, plus additional for sprinkling

2 large eggs, beaten together in a small bowl plus 1 more for an egg wash (1 egg mixed with 1 tablespoon water)

1 tablespoon vanilla extract

¼ cup (25 g) whole pecans

½ cup (85 g) dark chocolate chips

PREHEAT THE OVEN to 325°F (160°C). Line a 13-by-18-inch (33 by 46 cm) baking sheet (or two 9-by-13-inch (23 by 33 cm) baking sheets) with parchment or a silicone mat.

Put the flour, baking powder, salt, cinnamon, and oats in a mixing bowl and stir to combine. Set aside.

In a stand mixer fitted with a paddle attachment, cream the butter and sugar until light and fluffy (4 to 5 minutes on medium-low speed). Add the eggs and vanilla, turn the mixer off, and scrape the sides of the bowl with a rubber spatula. Turn the mixer back on and continue to beat until the egg mixture is light and fluffy (2 to 3 minutes). Add the flour mixture and mix with the butter on low speed, just until the flour is incorporated. (Do not overmix or your dough will be tough.) Fold in the pecans and chocolate chips with a rubber spatula.

Transfer dough onto a floured surface and roll it into a log about 12 inches (30 cm) long by 3 inches (7.5 cm) wide. (Or two logs 6 inches (15 cm) long each.) Place the log on the lined baking sheet, and flatten it slightly with your hands. Brush the top with the egg wash and sprinkle with sugar. Bake in the preheated oven until firm and lightly browned, 15 to 20 minutes. Remove from oven, reduce the temperature to 225°F (110°C), and allow the log to cool. Once cooled, slice crosswise into pieces between ½ to ¾ inch (12 mm to 2 cm) thick. Return the cut pieces to the baking sheet and bake until the edges of the biscotti become dry and crispy, about 30 minutes more. Remove from oven and allow to cool on the baking sheet or transfer to a cooling rack. Serve immediately or store in an airtight container for up to a week.

CHOCOLATE SOUFFLÉ

Whenever I see a chocolate soufflé on a restaurant menu, no matter how full I am or how much I'm working on my diet, I have to order one—I just cannot resist these things. I can't think of a more sophisticated dessert, nor one that is more satisfying (and fun) to eat. A lot of people pour crème anglaise over the top, but I prefer soufflés on their own, so nothing distracts from the textural contrast between the outside and inside: the crunchy caramelized edges on top against that rich, fluffy interior. A proper soufflé isn't hard to make at home, it just requires a bit of precision. The egg whites need to be whipped with absolutely no yolk in them (even a trace will prevent the meringue from forming properly), and after the ramekins are filled, it's very important to first level the soufflés with a paring knife, and then make a tiny, clean indentation between the filling and ramekin edge, which will allow the soufflé to rise properly.

Makes 5 soufflés

1 cup (240 ml) milk

¼ cup (50 g) granulated sugar

5 large eggs, separated, both whites and yolks reserved (make sure there is no trace of yolk in the whites)

2 tablespoons all-purpose flour

2 tablespoons cornstarch

1 teaspoon vanilla extract

3 ounces (85 g) good-quality dark chocolate (60–75%), chopped into small chunks

Butter, at room temperature, for the ramekins

2 tablespoons granulated sugar, plus additional as needed for coating the ramekins

Confectioners' sugar, for dusting

Special equipment: five 6-ounce ramekins

Recipe continues

Sweets

PREHEAT THE OVEN to 400°F (205°C).

In a small pot, whisk the milk, sugar, egg yolks, flour, cornstarch, and vanilla extract, then bring to a boil over medium heat. Cook for 3 minutes, scraping the bottom of the pan with a rubber spatula, until it reaches a thick, pudding-like consistency.

Transfer to a large bowl, then add the chopped dark chocolate and let it sit for about 1 minute before mixing well with a wooden spoon (the heat from the milk and egg yolk mixture will melt the chocolate). Once the chocolate is fully integrated and the mixture is smooth, place a sheet of plastic wrap directly on the surface so there's no air in between the plastic wrap and the chocolate mixture.

Use a brush to lightly coat the insides of the ramekins with butter, making sure you go all the way to the top so that none of the surface area is left bare. (Otherwise your soufflé will not rise properly.)

Once all the ramekins are thoroughly buttered, put a good amount of granulated sugar in each ramekin (enough to cover the bottom by ¼ inch), then swirl each one so that the sugar coats the sides as well. (You can place another ramekin under the one you are swirling to catch any sugar that doesn't adhere.)

Clean a mixing bowl and the whip or beater attachments of a stand mixer with hot water, then wipe both down with vinegar to ensure there is no fat adhering to them. Place the egg whites in the bowl and whip or beat them on high until soft peaks form, about 30 minutes, then rain in the 2 tablespoons granulated sugar until they become stiff peaks.

Take one-third of the meringue and whisk it into the chocolate base until completely smooth. Then add another third of the meringue and gently fold it in with a rubber spatula. Add the final third of the meringue and gently fold it in. Fill the ramekins with the chocolate meringue up to the top edge, using either a large spoon or a pastry bag. Gently tap each ramekin on the counter after it is filled to break up any air pockets. Level each ramekin with a paring knife, then place your thumb and index finger together, as if you were pinching salt. Place the index finger on the outside of the ramekin, and the thumb just inside the ramekin; the pads of your fingers should meet on top of the ramekin rim. Apply pressure on the thumb on the inside of the ramekin as you turn the ramekin around to complete the circle, so the rim is completely clean.

Place the ramekins on a cookie sheet and bake in the preheated oven for 9 to 10 minutes, until the soufflés have risen about 2 to 3 inches (5 to 7.5 cm) above the rim, and there is a nice golden crust.

Remove from the oven, dust the tops with confectioners' sugar, and serve immediately.

HAZELNUT AND BROWN BUTTER CAKE

When I was at L'Impero, we had these amazing pastry chefs, Heather and Jerry, who had this hazelnut cake on the menu. They would make it in sheets, trim the corners to create perfectly shaped portions for guests, and then leave piles of the unsellable edges on the shelf in their station for the rest of the staff to snack on. Eventually I had to beg them to take it off the menu because I just couldn't resist it, it was that ridiculously good. Once in a blue moon I'll still make this . . . when I'm feeling thin.

Note: This cake can be made gluten-free by substituting a gluten-free flour for the all-purpose in the same ratio. It's not quite the same, but still really, really good.

Makes one 10-inch (25 cm) cake; serves about 12

1 cup (2 sticks) unsalted butter, plus more for greasing the cake pan

⅔ cup (235 g) whole, shelled hazelnuts

¾ cup (95 g) all-purpose flour or gluten-free flour

3 cups (300 g) confectioners' sugar, plus more for dusting

1 pinch salt

1 cup (245 g) egg whites (from about 8 large eggs)

IN A SAUCEPAN, melt the butter over medium heat and continue to cook it until the butter turns brown and smells quite nutty, being careful not to let it burn, 10 to 15 minutes. Remove from heat, transfer to a heatproof dish (to prevent the butter from burning in the pot) and let cool to almost room temperature.

Meanwhile, preheat the oven to 350°F (175°C). Butter the bottom of a 10-inch (25 cm) round cake pan and line the bottom of the pan with parchment paper. Spread the hazelnuts on a baking sheet and toast them in the oven until lightly browned and fragrant, 10 to 15 minutes. Let the hazelnuts cool, but leave the oven on.

Remove about ¼ cup (35 g) of the nuts and chop them finely by hand. Grind the rest of the toasted nuts in a food processor until finely ground.

Sift the flour, confectioners' sugar, and salt together into a large bowl. Add the ground nuts and whisk to combine. Add the egg whites and whisk them together with the dry ingredients. Slowly pour in the melted butter, whisking constantly until the ingredients are completely incorporated and no butter is floating on top.

Pour the batter into the prepared pan and sprinkle the top with the reserved chopped nuts. Bake until the cake feels solid but the top still gives slightly when touched, 40 to 45 minutes. Let the cake cool in the pan for about 10 minutes before inverting it onto a serving plate. Just before serving, dust the top with some sifted confectioners' sugar. Serve immediately while warm. (Leftover will keep at room temperature for a day or two.)

WHOOPIE PIES

My father was from an old New England family in Maine—we are descendants of Roger Conant, who founded Salem, Massachusetts—and several times a year we would go there to visit my grandfather and my step-grandmother Marion. My recollections of our Thanksgiving trips are tainted by memories of freezing in the car on the drive up, but my summer memories are still vivid and fond: fresh lobster, boiled new potatoes—grown by my grandfather and cooked with plenty of butter—and whoopie pies. Mainers love their whoopie pies—it's the official "state treat"—and while you can now find them across the country in all sorts of variations, this recipe is an ode to the traditional New England version that I remember from those visits: little chocolate cakes bound by a filling of buttercream and Marshmallow Fluff.

Note: The filling is super sticky, so I strongly recommend using a pastry bag (or a ziptight bag with a corner cut off) to pipe it. Or, if you use a spoon instead, keep a bowl of warm water nearby to rinse with in between filling each pie.

Makes about 30 small pies

FOR THE CAKES:

¾ cup (1½ sticks/170 g) unsalted butter, at room temperature

1½ cups (300 g) granulated sugar

1 large egg

1½ teaspoons vanilla extract

3 cups (375 g) all-purpose flour

¾ cup (70 g) unsweetened cocoa powder

2 teaspoons baking soda

¾ teaspoon salt

1½ cups (360 ml) buttermilk

FOR THE FILLING:

1½ cups (3 sticks/340 g) unsalted butter, softened

3 cups (375 g) confectioners' sugar

3 cups (370 g) Marshmallow Fluff

1 tablespoon vanilla extract

MAKE THE CAKES: Preheat the oven to 350°F (175°C).

In an electric mixer fitted with a paddle attachment, cream the butter and granulated sugar on low speed until light and fluffy, about 5 minutes. Add the egg and vanilla and mix until well incorporated, scraping the sides with a rubber spatula as you go.

Sift together the flour, cocoa powder, baking soda, and salt, then add one-third of the flour mixture to the butter and egg mixture, followed by one-third of the buttermilk. Continue alternating the flour mixture and the buttermilk, mixing with the paddle and scraping the sides down as you go, until all the ingredients have been added and incorporated.

Line 2 baking sheets with parchment paper or a silicone mat, then add 2 to 3 tablespoons scoops of batter, spaced 3 inches (7.5 cm) apart on the baking sheet. Bake in the preheated oven for 8 to 10 minutes (test for doneness by pressing the middle of a cake; it should bounce back and not feel dry). Remove from the oven and transfer to a wire rack to cool. Repeat with the remaining batter until all shells have been baked.

Make the filling: While the cakes are cooling, combine the butter, confectioners' sugar, Marshmallow Fluff, and vanilla in the bowl of an electric mixer with a paddle attachment. Cream together the ingredients on low to medium-low until smooth and incorporated.

When the cakes are completely cooled to room temperature (it is important to cool them completely so the filling doesn't melt when it is added), line the cakes in two rows, one row of cakes flat side up and the other round side up.

Using a piping bag or a ziptight bag with a small piece cut on a diagonal from one of the corners, pipe 1 to 1½ tablespoons filling on the cakes with the flat sides up. Once all of the flat sides are filled, place the unfilled round-side-up cakes on top to create sandwiches. Serve immediately.

ZWETSCHGENKUCHEN (GERMAN PLUM CAKE)

When I lived in Germany, I worked for a time at a bakery in Bavaria where, during the summer, they made a traditional plum tart that blew me out of the water. The tart itself was very thin, with a nice crust on the bottom and a top that was super moist from absorbing the custard that was layered above it with caramelized plums cooked on top. My favorite part was always the sweet spot where the tart and custard meet. In Bavaria, the tart was referred to as *zwetschgen-kuchen* (for the variety of plums that were used), elsewhere it is called *pflaumenkuchen* (plum cake), and close variations of this recipe go by other names throughout Germany and Austria. Call it whatever you like; it's delicious in every language. (While you can make this tart any time of year, it's best when plums are at their peak.)

Makes one 8-inch tart

Tart Dough

⅓ cup plus 1 tablespoon confectioners' sugar

1 cup plus 1 tablespoon all-purpose flour

¼ cup unsalted butter, cold, thinly sliced

2½ tablespoons beaten egg

Scant 1 teaspoon ice water

Using a stand mixer fitted with a paddle attachment, add the sugar, the flour, and the butter to the bowl and mix on low speed until the ingredients come together in a way that resembles a crumble topping, with the dry ingredients coating chunks of butter. Add the egg and water and continue to mix on low speed until just combined. (Do not overmix.) Wrap the dough with plastic wrap and refrigerate for several hours.

Custard Filling

½ cup softened butter

½ cup powdered sugar

½ teaspoon granulated sugar

1½ teaspoons lemon zest

¼ teaspoon kosher salt

1 whole + 2 teaspoons large eggs

1 tablespoon whole milk

⅔ cup all-purpose flour

Using an electric mixer fitted with a paddle attachment, combine the butter, powdered sugar, granulated sugar, lemon zest, and salt and mix on medium-low speed until ingredients are creamed (about 4 to 5 minutes). Add the egg and the milk, scraping the sides of the bowl with a rubber spatula as you go. Add the flour and continue to mix until the flour has just disappeared. Set aside while you prepare the plums.

Recipe continues

Caramel Plums

½ cup granulated sugar

¼ cup corn syrup

¼ cup white verjus (or white wine)

3 black plums, ripe but not soft, halved and pits removed

In a large sauté pan, combine the sugar and corn syrup. Cook over medium heat until lightly caramelized. (Do not stir; gently swirl the pan.) Carefully add the verjus to dissolve the sugar, then reduce the heat to low.

Add the plum halves, cut side down, and cook on low heat for 10 minutes. Flip so they are face-up and cook for another 10 minutes, until the plums are soft but not falling apart. (If syrup starts reducing and caramelizing, deglaze with a little warm water.)

Remove the pan from the heat and let the plum halves rest until they are cool enough to cut into quarters, lengthwise. Reserve the juices.

Assemble the Tart

Preheat the oven to 350°F (175°C).

Roll out the tart dough ⅛ inch (5 mm) thick, then drape it over the tart pan, using leftover dough to press it into the sides. Level the top with a rolling pin, then prick the dough a few times with a fork. Bake the tart for 10 minutes, then remove it from the oven and let it cool.

Once the tart shell has cooled, spread the custard filling over the crust and arrange the plum segments over the top in a circular shape. Bake at 350°F for about 25 minutes, until there is a slight browning on the edges of the plums, where the skin and flesh meet. Remove the tarts from the oven, brush the plums with the reserved plum-cooking syrup, then return to the oven for 5 more minutes. Cool to room temperature, unmold, and serve.

SUMMER COMPOTE

This is a recipe I've used for years, in the restaurants and at home, as an accompaniment with cheeses. It's now also made its way onto the table when we do a Turkish breakfast at home—this compote with a little feta and *Gözleme* (page 200) is a grand slam.

Note: You can substitute whatever berries or stone fruit you have, in the same proportions, so feel free to experiment with what you have on hand or what is in season.

Makes 2 cups (470 g)

2 tablespoons sugar

1 cup (105 g) fresh cherries, pitted

¾ cup (110 g) fresh blueberries

¾ cup (105 g) fresh blackberries

¾ cup (125 g) fresh raspberries

Zest of ½ lemon plus 1 teaspoon lemon juice

Pinch salt

PUT THE SUGAR IN A SHALLOW SAUCEPAN set over medium heat and allow it to melt and caramelize, 7 to 9 minutes. Add the cherries, blueberries, blackberries, and raspberries and stir to coat the fruit with the sugar. Continue to cook on medium heat while the fruit releases its juices and then the liquid reduces, about 15 minutes more. When the mixture has reduced to a fruity syrup, remove from heat and stir in the lemon zest and juice and the salt. Place the pot in a bowl of ice water to cool, then transfer to a Mason jar and keep in the refrigerator for up to 1 week or until ready to use.

Coda

Maturity is not for the faint of heart. It's humbling. In the kitchens of my restaurants today, there's a new generation of young chefs, hungry as I once was to show the world what they can do, who are struggling to be heard through their food, as I once did. When I work with these younger chefs, I try to mentor them not only in cooking technique, but also in the tactics that I've learned are crucial to having a long career in this industry, the same ones the people like Mo Collins from the Sea Loft schooled me in: preparedness, discipline, and keeping a cool head. It's poignant to see these young chefs strive for what I did earlier in my career, with the same hunger that I once had: to have their food really say something to the world.

Maturity also means, hopefully, finally settling into oneself. In my case, while I still enjoy being around the energy and creativity of a restaurant kitchen, it has meant coming back to where my love of food began: at home. Over the past few years, I've spent a lot of time with my mother and my aunts, picking their brains about the food they grew up with, and bringing the dishes and flavors of my childhood back into my cooking. It's not just nostalgia—it's a full-circle return to an appreciation of all that cooking and eating symbolized in my childhood, and a desire to re-create that now with my own family. If there's one thing that I've learned, it's that food will always be more to me than something to eat. I hope that in sharing these recipes with you, I've helped you create special moments to share with your own family, too.

Peace, love, and pasta,
—Scott

I want to first thank the writer Caitlin Leffel; this book would never have gotten done if not for her incredible talent and dedication. I thank you dearly.

Maria Pallon and Irene Chiang, Jacob Vergara and Jackie Cecil; Daniel Tackett and Luis "Chepy" Cajamarca: I love you all and appreciate you beyond words. Thank you for all you do.

My business manager, Ken Slotnick at AGI; my agent, Josh Bider; and the rest of the WME team—Jeff Googel, Jon Rosen, Miles Gidaly, literary agent Eve Attermann, and Sam Birmingham.

My good friend Ken Goodman: You're so awesome.

Holly Dolce and Shannon Kelly, my editors, and the rest of the team at Abrams, thank you for believing in this book; and copyeditor Sarah Scheffel, for making the words perfect.

The *Chopped* and *Chopped Sweets* crew: Linda, Amy, and Vivian, all the producers, Michael Pearlman, Sean King, and the entire camera crew.

Everyone at the Food Network: Courtney White, Lynn Sadofsky, Neil Regan, and Todd Weiser; Irika Slavin, Lauren Mueller, Sierra Gray.

Over my years of cooking and being involved in food, I have had so many incredible people come into my life, a complete list of which is too long to attempt here. Some have mentioned something in passing that has stuck with me, some have showed me something important that I've never forgotten, some have simply given me a reason to ponder after a talk . . . no matter the situation, you have all had a profound effect on me. And for that I thank you all, but to name just a few:

Bobby Flay for all his incredible talent, insight and decisiveness. Il Capo!

Guy Fieri, for his generous heart. Alex Guarnaschelli (ICAG), Aarón Sánchez, Marcus Samuelsson, Tiffani Faison, Marc Murphy, Maneet Chauhan, Amanda Freitag, Chris Santos, Geoffrey Zakarian, Scott Savlov, Beau Mac, Lorenzo Boni, Michael Symon, Lee Schrager, Betty Park, Michael Voltaggio, Adam Sobel, Jackie Olensky, Sara Nahas Hormi, Marcela Valladolid, Alex Stratta, Mike Pirolo, Nina Compton, Miles Angelo, Dean Fearing, Norman Van Aken, Andrew Zimmern, David Sellers, Paride Guerra, Roberto De Angelis, Salvatore Esposito, Robbie Vorhaus, Ben Ford, Matt Adlard, Cliff Crooks, Gregory Alan, Jamie DeRosa, Vic Garrets, Rick Tramonto, Aaron May, Zac Young, Carla Hall, Eric Miller, Cesare Casella, Frank and Frank, Bob Grimes, Eric Weinberg, Jimmy Bradley, Ken Oringer, Jamie Bissonnette, Nick Stellino, Jeff Mauro, Bob Agahi, Anne Burell, Michael Lomonaco, Todd English, Josh Capon, Jet Tila, Paul Stanley, Jeff Tascarella, Joe Murphy, Joey Campanaro, Jackie Rothong, Andrew Essex, Shea Gallante, Demetrio Zavala, Tom Black, Frank Prisinzano, Christian Petroni, Sam Mason, Nancy Silverton, Richard Sandoval, Tom Valenti, Michael Mina, the Bromberg brothers, David Myers, Roy Choi, Charlie Palmer, Jonathan Waxman, Rita Jammet, Robert Irvine, Gavin Kaysen, Sam Fox, Bertha González, Susan Feniger, Carnie Wilson, Dan Langan, Evan Funke, Rob Gentile, Curtis Stone, Mary Sue Milliken, Marc Forgione, Suzanne Goin, Pino Luongo, Mark Tarbell, Herb Karlitz, Duff Goldman, Jason Smith, Sam Kass, Missy Robbins, Nobu, Drew Nieporent, Mauro Uliassi, and many, many, many more. And to all the young chefs and competitors I've had the pleasure of meeting: You all inspire me and I thank you for moving the chains forward. I learn from you daily.

The restaurant teams: too many to name, but thanks to every single one of you.

And finally, to my family, by whom I am inspired, have always been inspired, and will continue to be in the future.

Index

Index

Editor: Shannon Kelly
Designer: Heesang Lee
Production Manager: Anet Sirna-Bruder

Library of Congress Control Number: 2021932553

ISBN: 978-1-4197-4736-6
eISBN: 978-1-64700-054-7

Printed and bound in the United States
10 9 8 7 6 5 4 3 2 1

Abrams books are available at special discounts when purchased
in quantity for premiums and promotions as well as fundraising or
educational use. Special editions can also be created to specification.
For details, contact specialsales@abramsbooks.com or the address
below.

ABRAMS The Art of Books
195 Broadway, New York, NY 10007
abramsbooks.com